SPIRITUAL LETTERS

OF

EDWARD KING, D.D.

Emary Grantham.

E. Lincoln

SPIRITUAL LETTERS

OF

EDWARD KING, D.D.

LATE LORD BISHOP OF LINCOLN

EDITED BY

REV. B. W. RANDOLPH, D.D.

Canon of Ely and
Principal of Ely Theological College

A. R. MOWBRAY & CO. LTD.
LONDON: 28, Margaret Street, Oxford Circus, W.
OXFORD: 9, High Street

MILWAUKEE, U.S.A.: The Young Churchman Company

First Impression, November, 1910

INTRODUCTION.

EDWARD KING, the writer of these letters, was the son of the Archdeacon of Rochester, the Ven. Walter King, and grandson of the Bishop of Rochester, Dr. King, who held that See during the first quarter of the nineteenth century. He was born at Stone, December 29, 1829, and after being privately educated by tutors, he went to Oriel College, Oxford, and took his degree in 1851. After a short period of travel he was ordained in 1854 by Bishop Wilberforce to the Curacy of Wheatley, the village at the foot of the hill leading up to Cuddesdon. That he never lost his love for Wheatley and for the charm of village life the letters in this little volume abundantly testify. It was the same year in which the Theological College at Cuddesdon was founded. Four years later, in 1858, King became Chaplain of that Institution, when the Rev. Alfred Pott (afterwards Archdeacon of Berkshire) was Principal, and Henry Parry Liddon was Vice-Principal.

In 1863, on the death of the Rev. W. H. Swinney (who had succeeded Mr. Pott in 1859), King was made Principal. During his tenure of office, first as Chaplain and then as Principal, the College was from time to time the object of considerable suspicion; and though the attacks made on it by Mr. Golightly and others are now happily forgotten, it was no easy task to which King had been called.

Under all the strain of controversy, however, he kept quietly on, exercising an altogether unique influence over the students, and setting a standard in regard to the devotional life and ideals of Theological Colleges, which has profoundly influenced the English Church. His lectures and addresses were full of deep spiritual power, and made a lasting impression on successive generations of men.

In 1873 Mr. Gladstone nominated Canon King to the Regius Professorship of Pastoral Theology at Oxford, with a Canonry of Christ Church annexed. The ampler opportunities which this position afforded him were taken advantage of, and he became in a very few years the paramount religious influence in Oxford, exercising an extraordinary fascination over all kinds of undergraduates, and honoured and loved also by the senior members of the University.

On the resignation of Bishop Wordsworth of Lincoln early in the year 1885, Mr. Gladstone recommended King as his successor, and he was consecrated on S. Mark's Day in St. Paul's Cathedral—Dr. Bickersteth being consecrated to the See of Exeter at the same time—in the presence of a vast congregation. It was on this occasion that Dr. Liddon preached one of his most memorable sermons, and anticipated for his friend an Episcopate which would rank "hereafter with those which, in point of moral beauty, stand highest on the roll of the later English Church—with Andrewes, with Ken, with Wilson, and with Hamilton."

How completely this prediction has been fulfilled all the world knows. The Bishop enjoyed an Episcopate of twenty-five years (all but seven weeks), and died on March 8, 1910.

The letters in this volume have been selected by the present writer out of those which many kind friends of the Bishop have been good enough to send him, or from those which he has himself at various times received.

He desires to express his grateful thanks to those who have entrusted him with letters. His design has been to give to the world a small volume of *Spiritual Letters*; he has, therefore, somewhat rigorously excluded all such letters as would not naturally be found in such a category, or which might more properly be included in a Biography.

The first nineteen letters were all written to the same correspondent, who, as a boy at Wheatley, began his acquaintance with King in 1857, and who kept up a yearly correspondence with him from that date till 1909.

The other letters are of a more miscellaneous character, and it has been found difficult to arrange them very satisfactorily in order of subjects. The Fragments at the end, which are taken for the most part out of longer letters, will not be thought the least precious part of the volume. Simplicity, tenderness, sympathy and love—combined with deep spiritual insight—these are the notes which seem to dominate every one of these letters, while ever and anon there are flashes of that quiet humour and playfulness which those who knew the Bishop will recognise as one of the most delightful and never-failing traits of his beautiful, inspiring, and uplifting character.

B. W. RANDOLPH.

THE ALMONRY, ELY.
Feast of St. Hugh of Lincoln, 1910.

LIST OF CONTENTS.

CONTENTS.

BISHOP KING'S SPIRITUAL LETTERS.

I.

TO A PUPIL TEACHER—GROWTH IN CHARACTER.

STONE, 1858.

Thank you for all your letters. You know I have had much to think of lately; indeed, at such times it seems more proper to be quiet in thought than to speak or write much.

It is a time to learn rather than to teach.

I hope you have not (or rather *I* have not) given very much trouble to your family about the house. I hope, if all is well, to return on Thursday. I shall be very glad to be near you all once more. This world is so full of changes, C——, that we cannot tell how long we may be together. I think it would be a great pleasure to me if God should see fit to leave me near you until your character is firmly settled in the right way. It would give me great pleasure, though I do not deserve such a reward. If only you are really good, humble and earnest, I will willingly be content that God may teach you, protect you in soul and body, and form your whole mind according to His Will, and bless you in yourself, and if He spares you in your future work. This is ever, C——, the daily and earnest prayer of one who, through much weakness, loves you dearly for Christ's sake.

Yours affectionately.

God bless you all!

II.

TO THE SAME—KNOWLEDGE AND WISDOM.

STONE, DARTFORD, *March* 1, 1859.

I am very sorry to hear that your mother is ill. I hope one of you will write and tell me how she is.

I have not written to any of you because I am afraid I may have already given you more trouble than is good for you from my own weak health, and I am afraid that I shall make you too sad, when you ought to be happy and cheerful.

We leave all to our God, Who loves us far better even yet be spared us, but the doctors say we must expect the trial to be a long one.

We leave all to our God, who loves us far better than we love ourselves or one another. I am trying to learn what I have often said, "Thy will be done."

I trust you are going on well. Be pure, honest, humble, earnest. Strive by reading, with prayer and meditation, to obtain "the mind of Christ." Get all the knowledge you can, labour to become a perfect master of all the subjects you may have to teach.

You must have this *knowledge*, but always remember that knowledge and *wisdom* are different things.

"Knowledge is proud that she knows so much,
Wisdom is humble that she knows no more."

Look out S. James iii. 17. Remember it when your blackboard and chalk are ready. Remember me to R. R. and all your family.

God bless you all! I am, my very dear C——,
Yours very affectionately.

III.

TO THE SAME—ON THE BIBLE.

STONE, *July* 30, 1859.

Thank you for your two letters. I am not sorry that you have met with an opponent while you are yet with us. At the same time I would advise you not to talk more than is necessary with such persons. It is much easier to throw dirt than to wash it off. I shall be very glad to talk over all that he has said. One or two things I may mention now.

A.

1.—Your friend says that he has

(*a*) *Studied* } the Bible and does not
(*b*) Thought over } believe it.

Now, giving him credit for having done this, I am not the least surprised that he does not believe it, unless he can add that he has (*c*) *Done* (*i.e.*, put into practice) *all that he has read!*

If any man will DO His Will, he shall know of the doctrine, whether it be of God (S. John vii. 17).

2.—If your friend is now *forty years* old, was good as a *boy* and *young man*, and has really for the last twenty years with prayer and fasting studied the Bible, putting INTO PRACTICE AT ONCE all he read, and still does not believe, I shall be glad to know who he is that I may hear more about him.

But even if he has done all this I shall not be shaken.

We sometimes find a calf with two heads, or a child born with no arms.

So there are extraordinary kinds of *minds*, which puzzle us, but which we *know quite well* are not the regular *intended pattern*, but in fact they are *mental monsters*, just like the calf or the child.

B.

1.—With regard to Cain's wife, you are quite right in thinking that the Bible does not *profess* to contain a full account of everything. It is a guide Book for fallen man, pointing out the way back to eternal happiness. *The Way*—that is, *Christ* our Saviour.

2.—If you were to ask me to tell you how to go to Oxford, would you think me a wise guide if I were to tell you where *all* the *roads would lead you which branch out of the way* you want to go. I should have to *mention* them to tell you *to pass on*, but that would be enough.

So you must not expect the Bible will satisfy your

curiosity, and, indeed, if you believe our God to be our *Father* you will not expect that His love would allow us to be so much bothered, *for good*.

I shall be very glad to talk this over with you again. You see, C——, these questions are only to be really answered by those *old deep quiet thoughts*. It is for this reason that I want you to *think*.

C.

1.—When your friend says the Bible is *only like* any other history,

May I ask:

(1) What other histories he has read?
(2) Which of these are as old as the Bible?
(3) Which of them contain so many wonderful types and prophecies?

The children are talking to me while I am writing, so I must stop. I hope you will enjoy your holidays. I hope to be back Saturday, the 6th.

God bless you, my dear C——. Give my love to J.

Yours very affectionately.

IV.

TO THE SAME—ON SAYING "NO."

WOODSIDE, DARTFORD, *January* 10, 1860.

Many thanks for your good wishes. I hope you will always keep up the same warmth of heart, but you will find the world makes many cold.

I am very glad that you have had such a good holiday. It is not so easy to live well out in the world as it is at Cuddesdon.

I am not surprised, at least not very much, at your not being at church. At the same time, I expect C—— did not feel quite right, and possibly thought he was wrong, and so you really were, my dear C——. But you see how hard it is to live in the world *with kind people who* are not very religious, and not to give up one's own time, and yet not to offend. One of the best ways to say "*No*" without offending people is to be free from *selfishness*. If you are always ready to do anything for anybody, when you say "*No*" people will understand that it is not want of goodwill on your part, but from real *principle*, because you do not think it right to do what they ask you to do. Don't forget this selfishness, *i.e.*, *pleasing oneself* is often the root from which the difficulty of saying "*No*" springs.

If you had cleaned *Mr. A.'s* boots, held his horse in a snow storm, posted his letters in a pouring rain, given him the sugar out of your tea, waited two hours for him without a *growl*, you might, after *years* of such conduct, have said "*No*" without any danger of giving offence. The sugar, the boots and the letters are all in your power. But the "*No*" BY ITSELF is often really too much. But then observe it is *our* fault that it is too much. It might have *been within our* power.

But you are tired of this, I can see.

The doves came quite safe. I take them to-morrow to my brother's children.

God bless you.

V.

TO THE SAME—ON WORSHIP.

ST. LEONARDS, *January* 17, 1863.

I have had such a quantity of letters to write, and have been so much put out of my way by the incessant eating and drinking which goes on here, that I have never written to you to thank you for your letter from Addington, and I am very glad to hear a good account of you all, and to know that you had been helping to keep up the services (I am not going to write you a *sermon*), but I advise you sometimes to consider the two views (or uses) of worship:—

(1) To ask for things for ourselves.

(2) To render the glory which is due to God.

People do not think enough about the second point. They only pray or go to church when they want something. The devil tries to make them think it would be an act of pride to offer God anything, but He says plainly: "Whoso *offereth* Me thanks and praise he honoureth Me."

And we know among ourselves how pleased a mother is with a present from her *children*, and so will you be just as much pleased by the attention from your children as I have been by all your loving affection and attention for the last six years to myself.

Don't forget then that it is a *poor selfish* thing only to have services when we want to get something. It ought always to be kept up as much as we can here, and really always in heaven.

But you know all this, my dear Charlie, just as well as I do. I only fear that the ignorant *mass* of half-hearted Christians at —— may make you doubt these *truths*.

Your most grateful and affectionate.

VI.

TO THE SAME—NOW BECOME A STUDENT AT CULHAM TRAINING COLLEGE.

St. Leonards, *January* 25, 1863.

I am afraid you have no second post at Culham, so that this will not be ready for you on your arrival, as I wished. However, it will not be displeasing to you, I dare say, in the morning in the midst of your new friends.

Many thanks for your letter. I am very glad you are through your examination. No doubt you are all the better without the first class, and so am I, as it saves me my ten pounds! But I mean to give you half, and will send you £5 as soon as I get back. This will help for the books, etc. If I forget please remind me.

And so now you are really at college!

I hardly know what to say to you. However, go on in your old way. Don't be in a hurry to change for new ways, which others would persuade you are better or more independent, or more telling in the world. Beware of smart dealing, swaggering, loud talking, showing off your knowledge, thinking yourself a *great government man!!* etc. All these things are simply *poor*. Pray don't be tempted by them, my dearest C——. You must be careful at first with whom you make friends. There are no doubt some very nice fellows, but there are sure to be some of both sorts, and the bad ones are generally first to make friends.

Don't fall into the so-called little acts of dishonesty in regard to lessons, etc., but treat your masters as you have always treated me. Do not be disappointed if they do not take much notice of you; it may be all the better for you.

Make good use of your opportunities for learning; work away. Drawing is a useful thing, and keep up your music. I need not add that you must keep from all real harm. Simply get out of the way of all bad conversation; go away from it; it is poison and contemptible. Don't stand it, but leave the fellows.

Keep to your services. The Holy Communion every Sunday I think you may do, and the rest as often as you can. A few years of discipline makes the rest of life much easier.

God bless you.

VII.

TO THE SAME—ON HUMILITY.

CUDDESDON, *Tuesday.*

I am indeed glad that you have got on so well. You see if you would but believe me you might save yourself much anxiety, instead of being afraid where no fear was. I should think about this if I were you, and while you keep up fresh and trembling all your old nervous humility, just throw yourself back on the fact that God made you what you are, and, therefore, do not fear failure or want of power.

You know I am a wretched shaky old thing frightened to death, but I try to get the better of it. I do think that perfect humility, being content to be anywhere where God places one, does cure a great deal of nervousness, and so leaves one's mind more free to do its work. . . . But come and see me, and I will finish my *sermon* then.

God bless you, and guide you, and fit you for His holy love.

I am, yours most affectionately.

VIII.

TO THE SAME—ON HOLIDAYS.

CUDDESDON, *June* 21, 1864.

In case I do not come over to-day, which I hope to do if I can, I write to say I should not urge you to take work in the holidays.

(1) You are not likely to be idle, and to fall into the danger of idleness.
(2) You will not learn much in a few weeks that you will not learn over and over again when you are at work.
(3) You will gain more by quietly resting and looking at your present work and future life, and by going about and seeing other people and their difficulties, and learning their thoughts of life.

[Cultivate] love for all that are in the dark, love for all in trouble—anxiety. The world is unsatisfying, and yet how much there is for us to do in it. All these sort of thoughts are very valuable. They are the cleansing and mending of our net, which can only be done in times of rest. So I should not urge you to get work; yet if you are bent upon it I shall wish you heartily success in it.

God bless you and keep you.

IX.

TO THE SAME—ON CONVERSION.

CUDDESDON, WHEATLEY, *February* 27, 1865.

I am dead tired and ought to be in bed, but I will not let another day go by without writing to you. Thank you for your affectionate letter. As for conversion, don't let that bother you. The fact is there are two sorts of conversion:—

(1) From a life of thoughtless sin to godliness.
(2) In a life of godliness to a closer walk with God.

The first, thank God, you know nothing of, nor do I, but the second we both practise, and need to practise every day. Do not be put out by this. You will see before long that their view of one conversion once for all does not practically do. They will sin again, and need fresh conversion.

I hope to come to you in the summer. I should enjoy a talk with you very much.

All goes on here well (thank God); the college is full and all work well. I have just got a new set of bellringers, which I am very glad of. Bellringers ought to be a godly set, nearly like choirmen. It only wants perseverance and to get the idea into people's heads, and then it will come.

I send you a card I have made for some of my young men, just to remind you of old days. Get some plan for Lent; read something. Now, good-night.

God bless you, and fill you with His wisdom and His holy love.

X.

TO THE SAME—THE GOSPEL LIFE.

VICARAGE, CUDDESDON, WHEATLEY,
September 12, 1865.

Pray do not think that you have given me needless worry. I cannot say that I am not anxious to see the temptations of the world safely conquered by you, but this anxiety is not more than anyone must have for their children in the faith, and I am sure you are going on far better than ninety-nine out of a hundred, but you know that I long to see a real and simple imitation of the Life we have shown to us in the Gospels. It seems to me that if people go on allowing themselves to shape their lives so much more by the circumstances of the world than by the Gospel, they will be in danger of disbelieving the truths of the Bible itself.

I am anxious to prove, if it please God, in my own life that the Gospels are true.

I know one must make a horrid mess of the matter, and be sorry not to be what you would like to be.

Still, that is a very different thing from not trying at all, and simply following with the mass.

All you want, my dear C——, is to keep on, on, on, and you will find the blessing some day even in this life, and I need not add in the next. God bless you, my dear child, and make your Sundays real *holy days*, not working days. You will gain more by so doing.

God bless and guide you, and love you.

XI.

TO THE SAME—ON THE BREAKING UP OF HOME.

OXFORD, *April* 8, 1865.

Just a line to thank you for your nice note. I can quite understand how you must feel the breaking up of the old home. After all, in spite of position, honour, money, there is something in the memory of home which speaks of a higher pleasure than those things can give us. It tells us, I think, of the true joy in the eternal home, to which, I trust, we are one by one being taken. The world certainly is not satisfying and must always be full of trouble, and division, and confusion. We must do our best in it, and with it, but our real life, and rest, and satisfaction is not to be looked for here, but above.

Take all the care of your health you can. I should be inclined to get help in teaching, so as to rest a little, and then go bravely on, and trust to God to order all for the best. We never can tell how it is to be.

I am always glad to hear of you, and you must look to me for a little news of the old country now.

God bless you and your friends. Wishing you all the holy joy and hope of Easter.

XII.

TO THE SAME—ON BLESSINGS IN THE CHURCH.

CUDDESDON VICARAGE, WHEATLEY,
April 16, 1868.

Thank you for your kind letter and invitation to come and see you. I should enjoy it very much, but I cannot get away very well. My sister is to be married (D.V.) next Tuesday, and we are all more or less in a muddle preparing for it, and then term begins again.

I am very thankful you can give such a good account of yourself and of your work. The Church has many enemies just now, and infidelity is making itself felt in high places, but I see no reason in that for fear; indeed, I rejoice because I believe it will make people think and look a little deeper into things, and then we shall, please God, win them back to the old way of the Church. People have gone wild these last fifteen years in England from liberty of thought, and now, poor things, they are beginning to see that they do not know what to think, and in a little time more will be glad of some quiet, simple, good, sensible people to guide them. Then we must be ready, C——, to do our best. England has been sadly ignorant of the Church it has possessed and upheld for the last 200 years. I am not sorry its sleepy foot is beginning to wake up, though it will cause some pain at first, and, perhaps, cause some to fall, but it had much better go through that, and we shall get on better after a bit. All these anxieties about the Establishment need not trouble you. It is too big a thing for you or me to have much to do with, or to try and change, but the Church existed for 300 years without being joined to the State, and could just as well exist again. It is very bad for the State, and I think wrong, unless it gives back all the property, to separate, but as far as the Church is concerned it will not be necessarily essentially injured. Simply, you need not worry about it.

The Church holds its powers from our Blessed Lord, not from the Queen or Parliament, and no man can take them away.

This is a long letter about the Church, because you used to say I never taught you anything about it. Now, dear C——, here is a *sermon* for you! But I will stop. I am very glad your school does well. The old high, quiet, simple, supernatural way is the most powerful, and the most peaceful, because it is independent of this world's offers. If people would make up their minds to go straight for the next world they might throw their hats up in this, and be bright and happy.

God bless you, dear child.

XIII.

TO THE SAME—ON HIS MARRIAGE.

CUDDESDON, WHEATLEY, *October* 11, 1868.

I have not had a moment to send you my best congratulations, and to wish you every blessing. I was quite surprised to hear it, but not the less glad. I know how hard it is to work on through life alone that I am quite glad to think you will have someone to take care of you. I hope you will have a happy and useful life together. If you both try and live to do God's Will you will be happy. God bless you! My dear C——, I will certainly (D.V.) come and marry you, and I will send you £20 for a wedding present to spend as you please. Tell your future wife she must promise to take great care of you, or I will not come and marry you.

Every blessing be with you both.

XIV.

TO THE SAME—ON MAKING PROGRESS.

FOLKESTONE, *October* 21, 1869.

This time I am the first to write! In fact, I am trying to turn over a new leaf, and really look upon letters as a duty; this is about the 210th I have written this vacation. I am afraid I shall fall back when term begins, so I will just write to you and have my *boast*. How are you, my dear child? I hope quite strong again, but write and say as I want to know. I was very glad to see you this summer, and to see you getting on so well, and more old and settled in ways of thought. Every year will, I hope, add to that. One gets wiser and less drawn away and put out by trifles, but it is difficult to realise the true value of souls and the reality of the great world to come in the midst of a business world or a world of pleasure. Here it is all pleasure, the dressing of the people is really wonderful. Poor things, they can have very little to think about. How is your school and your choir? I am trying to learn to sing *tenor*. I mean to practise this winter.

I go back to Cuddesdon to-morrow. Now, good-bye. Tell me how you are. Remember me most kindly to your wife. God bless you.

XV.

TO THE SAME—VILLAGE LIFE.

CUDDESDON VICARAGE, WHEATLEY,

July 22, 1871.

It is simply work that has prevented my writing, or perhaps I ought to say work and want of method. For a man of good business habits would, I fancy, find more time, but it is difficult to reduce spiritual work, and the heads and hearts of people, to the formal business rules of the world. Anyhow, whether by my fault or not, I find letter writing one of my greatest troubles.

I am very glad your school is doing well, and I am glad to see you have taken the children to see the beasts. Those little kindnesses do a great deal of good. Our school is not what I could wish it to be. This year the village was quite upset by scarlet fever, and the schools closed, so it is not fair to judge, but still it is not up to the mark. I hope, however, it will improve, for the master, I think, likes us, and is anxious to please. He is good at the organ, and, with the help of Mr. Eichbaum, the choir is very much improved. The services are quite pleasant now. We have had for nearly twelve months a children's service, at three, every Sunday afternoon. We sing a metrical Litany and then catechise them. We are doing the Acts of the Apostles, and this and a few hymns and prayers takes about fifty minutes.

The children are in the best part of the church, and we have no regular choir, so it is their own service, but several parents come and seem to like it. I like it myself very much. I enjoy talking to children. If you think you could have one I will send you one of our little Litany books.

I do not wonder, dear C——, at your feeling pressed by the conflict of opinions; but, thank God, I see no reason to change. I should very much like to have a walk and talk with you as of old. The old way of simple Christian brotherhood seems to me still to be the way. People get influenced by the world and selfish, and proud, and idle, and there are also so many bad people that one is apt to become suspicious, and disbelieve in people, and so to treat them with a kind of hard reserve. But that is no good; a full disinterested love always ready to help, always longing to help most in spiritual things. This is what is wanted to raise people from the sour, unbelieving, materialistic thoughts, which the rough struggle of life too often produces.

I have been obliged these last few years to spend the best of my time in reading, but if I should be free from the college I should go on in a parish just as we used to at Wheatley. That was a simple, unworldly affectionate life, and that is what we want. I do not think people are simple enough in their religious relations. I wish we could be more open and united in the use of the churches as houses of prayer and praise. I have done very little, alas! in the parish, but, thank God, a few enjoy very much being with us. The simple carter lads require to be surrounded with a constant flame of love to save them from the hardness which their life with the animals and rough men bring on them. Our dear country poor—for I feel more suited to them than others—require to be helped one by one. They are very ignorant, have very little time, work very hard, and often with poor food; they require a great deal of loving watchful sympathy. If it please God, I should rejoice to give myself wholly to spiritual work.

Sometimes I think I should still like to go over to Australia and work there, but I fear my health is not equal to much rough work, but we must see; no doubt it will be arranged for the best. Now I have sent you quite a long letter. Don't mind the difficulties of religious thought, and don't get out of heart, or hard, or selfish, or merely worldly-wise, but strive to live a life in union with God, and that will fill you with wisdom and love, and preserve in you that spiritual freshness which is so splendid in teaching the young.

God bless you, dear C——, and guide you and support you in your work.

XVI.

TO THE SAME—VILLAGE LIFE.

LINCOLN, *January* 8, 1895.

It seems only yesterday that you used to come down to my room with dear G. and J., and we used to sit and talk together. I don't know that I have ever been happier. I was thoroughly happy with you all at Wheatley. I ought to be very thankful for all God's great goodness to me. I did not think I should live so long. I think our way of looking at things was the right one. We saw where true happiness was to be found. I long to promote the same kind of spirit in our country parishes. The Lincolnshire people are very nice, strong-headed, deep-hearted, religious people. My happiest time is when I am confirming in the country parishes. That I enjoy immensely. Thank you so much for your prayers. I am sure it is that which has kept me on. I should have broken down long ago but for that. I must stop now. I forget we are not sitting over the fire at Wheatley. It was very nice, wasn't it? I hope you are able to keep the same spirit of simplicity and love round about you. Good-bye, my dear C——. Don't forget me in your prayers. With my love and blessing to you all.

XVII.

TO THE SAME—OLD AGE.

CHARD, *St. Peter's Day*, 1905.

In heart I feel just the same as when we were all at Wheatley together, with dear J. and G. and you and H. I often look back to those days with the greatest thankfulness and pleasure; we were all very happy.

Thank you so much for your kind letter. I was very glad to get it, and to hear that you are so comfortable and happy. I know you have given up the school, but I don't quite know what you are doing. Write and tell me, and what your children are doing. I should have been so glad to have seen you again if I had gone to Cuddesdon, but I could not go. I hear of Wheatley sometimes from James White. I had not heard of the death of ——. He and Joseph were good-living men. When I saw your black paper I was afraid you had lost your dear wife. Remember me to her. So many of one's old friends have passed away. I must soon think of retiring even if I live. I am very grateful to you for your prayers. Don't forget me now, for I need all the more help as I find my strength naturally failing me. I have indeed many reasons to be thankful to God for His great goodness to me through all these years. I am, thank God, free from pain and able to get through my work. Your letter pleased me very much, because there was a spirit of content and happiness which I was most glad to see, and the love for your flowers brought back the memory of our old walks. I still love flowers and birds as much as ever. All the education work is sadly altered. I look back to the old school days with increasing value.

Now, good-bye. God bless you, dear C——, and give you grace and peace to the end, and ever remember me in your prayers!

XVIII.

TO THE SAME—THE PSALMS.

LINCOLN, *January* 21, 1907.

I was very glad to hear from you again. I want to thank you very much for your last kind letter, so full of old affectionate memories. I thought of you when I read the account of Mr. G.'s death in a paper which his daughter sent me—such a nice account of a well-spent life. I was so thankful to see it; he was a very nice-dispositioned man, and apparently he kept the same to the last—humble, kind, true to his church, choirmaster, churchwarden, and fond of flowers. He always was a good man, we must try and follow him.

I am sorry you are bothered about the different schools of thought. It is partly that we are growing old (I am quite old!!), and so we must expect changes and new ways of looking at things, but do not let this worry you. I think you must have been reading something about the "New Theology" of Mr. C——. There is not much new in it. It seems to be Pantheism in its tendency. I should leave all that, if I were you, and keep to the old lines of the Church. I have found increasing comfort in the Psalms and in the collects of our Prayer Book. The collects for this week and the fifth Sunday after Trinity are very comforting when things seem to be going wildly. All is really under the eye and hand of God. I find reading a period of history and saying those collects a great comfort. You see what the world has gone through under God's hand. The 2nd Psalm is a great comfort, and the 29th Psalm, the 9th verse "The Lord sitteth above the water-flood," or "The Lord sat enthroned above the flood." Well, if He could guide the ark over that He can guide us now! To learn to trust in God is a great thing, and to keep asking God to teach us as in the 119th Psalm again and again.

You see, C——, I keep to the old way, and I find more and more how it supports and satisfies me. If I come your way I will certainly let you know, for I should very much like to see you again. Don't forget to pray for me. I pray for you every morning.

God bless you, and keep you, and guide you.

Yours affectionately.

XIX.

TO THE SAME—THE OLD WAYS.

September 8, 1909.

I am very sorry that I have been so long thanking you for your last kind letter. I find it very difficult now to do more than attend to important letters of business.

I am very glad to hear that you are keeping well, though I am sorry your wife is poorly. Good health is indeed a wonderful blessing. Many of your dear brothers have gone, and your sisters too. I look back to the life at Wheatley with the greatest pleasure, with all of you, and dear Mr. G.—he was a nice-minded man—there was a real bond of disinterested love between us all.

People now are trying to make themselves happy without religion, but it is a hollow, heartless kind of happiness, not worthy of the name. I believe the love of God must stand first, and then, in God, we can love one another. People want to have social security and comfort, but without religion, without the Church. We must hold fast to the old way of the love of God, and the love of one another as taught us in the Bible and the Prayer Book, and we want the Church for the sake of the ministry of the Word and Sacraments, by which God teaches us, and gives us His grace.

God bless you, dear C——, and guide you on to

the end, which is really the *great beginning!* Remember me in your prayers, as I do you, every day. God bless you and all like you.

XX.

TO AN ORDINAND—ON HIS PARTING FROM A FRIEND.

CUDDESDON, *March* 11, 1873.

I should have written last night, because I felt you must be a little silently sad. But, dearest child, it will all be right. The more we can throw our wills in with the great Will of God, which is being done by good people round us, the stronger our lives become; so it is much better that H. should carry out his father's wish, and that you should give up, rather than break off, and begin on your own independent wills.

And then, do let me assure you that the heart is of such immense capacity if we only give it up to God to discipline, that these woundings are rather *prunings* for greater beauty and richer fruit. Had you gone with your good friend it might have narrowed the circle of your love, and you would not have had the sense of freedom to love all who may be waiting to be won by you to Him through your real love for them. *Now* there is a sense of solitude, of sadness, but believe me that will be more, *infinitely more*, than filled by that which is to come. These acts of divine discipline are simply invitations to trust our hearts to *Him*. He says in them to the heart: "Open thy mouth *wide* and I *will fill* it." You will be more free, C. will be more free, not feeling you are bound together to his exclusion, and you may, I think, do a great work for dear H., if you can love him, and win him and make him love you; you will be helping another soul to realise what he believes but does not quite feel, the *unity of all in Christ*, and all the while your greater love for God will give you new capacities and power to love your old friend at Wantage more and more.

So, dearest child, there is a great work beginning for you.

May He Who made you and redeemed you sustain you to do *all* His Will. . . .

XXI.

TO THE SAME—ON BEGINNING HIS CLERICAL WORK.

CUDDESDON, *June* 19, 1873.

I cannot wait any longer without talking with you; it seems such a long time since we met, and all this last year you have been so much in my mind and heart that it is difficult just at present to get on. I thought of you all on Sunday, and I am very glad the good Eichbaum says you all got on so well. You had the hardest sort of preaching possible in preaching at the Union. Poor things, they are so divided in their interests, and often so hard. I am glad you did not forget the children. You must have felt it, I am sure, very much helping at the early Celebration—it is most wonderful. Every year I feel more and more unfit. It is a very great pleasure to me to think of you all at work. There is a very great opportunity for you. I am sure we must be full of hope—brave, self-sacrificing, victorious hope. To me, thank God, all these troubles of the intellect, and all our ecclesiastical and social anxieties, are full of hope. They are but, I believe, the pain and labour which will issue in the birth of more truth, more true liberty, more true union between man and nature, and man and God, a bringing us in all things nearer to *Him*. Only, dearest child, in all this we must keep quiet and steady in our personal union with Him. Whatever victories there may be for us we must remember to rejoice, "because our names are written in heaven," because by His loving overruling of our lives we are being drawn nearer to Him and to one another in Him. May He help us so to live out our separate lives here that we may live together hereafter.

God bless you and keep you.

XXII.

TO THE SAME—ON HIS HOLIDAYS AT HOME.

INNSBRUCK, *Sunday, August* 24th, 1873.

This is just one line to give you confidence, and help you to take a *steady aim on the First!* I know you will be rather bothered, dear man, as to what is really best, but, I think, you are quite right to go simply on and *shoot*. It would, I know, seem ungrateful to the opportunities your father has provided for you, and seem a little like setting yourself up, and all that, from which I know you would recoil, and then it will do you good in health to get another good turn in the fresh air away from schools and cottages, and to feel again the original freedom which you used to feel, and it will refresh you mentally, and be a change, and get you out of the pressure of work.

I am not saying all this out of false kindness, because, I think, it is telling you to do what you like (I love you too truly for that), but because I do value so highly a natural growth in holiness, a humble grateful acceptance of the circumstances God has provided for each of us, and I dread the unnatural, forced, cramped ecclesiastical holiness, which is so much more quickly produced, but is so human and so poor. Do not let me deceive you. I believe we need to be separated off from the world, only let us be gentle, and not rash in pushing ever nearer to Him. I do hope we shall never lose in England the true manly independent spirit which our clergy have.

There is a great deal in the foreign clergy which we should do well to copy, but there is a good deal also which we should be very foolish to envy, and most unwise to adopt. I had a very valuable talk with Döllinger about this. He was most clear about it. Now, I have always felt, dear man, that you may become by God's grace just one of the sort of priests that England wants. I need not tell you of the social manly gifts—you have got these. All I want to do is to beg you not to despise them and throw them away, but to raise them and devote them to the higher and more spiritual part of the priestly office. I have been rejoiced to see how everybody likes you, but all that must bring danger to you, and, unless *very* carefully watched, will end in a hollow popularity, loss of individuality, and self-contempt. Be on your guard, dear man, in all that side of the matter, and yet *don*'t throw it all up, and hang your head, and look like a *whipped pointer*. In spite of all I say, I expect you *won't* care for the shooting so much this year, and by degrees, I believe, you will give it quite up, and find that God has led you naturally to take a delight in higher things. Only go gradually, and, as far as possible, naturally, taking the circumstances God gives you, and trying to serve Him in them. Real love of God, real love of man, a real living for the world to come, a real humility; these are the great strong elements of the Christian life. You will say then: "Am I to go on shooting when I am a priest."

No, dear man, I could not recommend you. I have, of course, no sort of right to stop you, but I could not recommend you, as I do now, and for two reasons:—

(1) Because of the great mystery of the priesthood, and the greatness of the work it involves; and

(2) Because I hope you will by that time not really need it, or wish it, but be naturally interested in supernatural thoughts and works.

And now, dearest friend, only one word more. Forgive the troublesomeness of my love, and crumple all this, as I told you last year, and ram it to the very bottom of your gun, and blaze it at the first bird you see, and shout again in freedom: "There goes the old Principal"; and yet, when you have killed your bird and eaten it, digest also one or two of the thoughts which you may remember were on the paper that helped to kill the bird. Once more, good-bye. Enjoy a free, happy, homely holiday, and may He teach you and bless you, not according to the measure of my, but *His*, love. . . .

XXIII.

TO THE SAME—ON HIS ORDINATION TO THE PRIESTHOOD.

CHRIST CHURCH, OXFORD, *May* 30, 1874.

Thank you for thinking of me. I am so glad that again nothing has hindered God's good purpose for you, and that He is gradually unfolding to you His eternal love for you, and His choice of you to be so near Himself in His great work of restoring men. I hardly like to make any noise with my voice to one round whom I doubt not the angels will be gathering, and to whom God the Holy Spirit will come with new powers, to teach you and guide you to guide and teach others. My joy is to think that my dear and merciful Lord will take you. *Twenty* years ago to-morrow He took me in the same Church, and for *twenty years* He has put up with me, and never left me, nor let me wholly leave Him, but led me on till at least I can say, honestly, "There is none like Him," and honestly I can joyfully trust that He will do for you as He has for me, more than even I could ask or think. Yes, dearest friend, with all my sincere love for you, my greatest joy is to think now He will take you nearer to Himself. Only, dearest friend, do not measure your priesthood by mine. No, I have often told you I am not what you may all be, but this is making a noise. So, good-bye. Just simply give yourself to God, never mind what you *feel*, your being weary or excited, or put out by some trifles, but that will pass, and the great supernatural *fact* will remain.

God bless you, and make you a priest according to His own Will. . . .

XXIV.

TO THE SAME—ON READING.

LONDON, *January* 14, 1873.

I am afraid you may have been expecting to hear from me before this, when you were so kind as to write so really about yourself to me. And, indeed, dearest child, you ought to have heard if it had not been for my wretched laziness. Alas! I have given way so miserably to the excuses of a not strong body that I fear I have greatly missed the good I might have done if I had been more diligent with my letters. I am trying to do better, and, if it please God to spare me to recover this, or rather, perhaps, not to add to it, I should be most thankful.

You say yourself, dear friend, that you suffer from temptation to idleness, *i.e.*, idleness in *reading*, for I should not think you were ever an idle, lazy, lethargic man, and so I should think it would be well to keep the point clear. If I am right—I mean I think you will find the work of visiting, preaching, teaching in school classes not difficult to you. Neither will you be much tempted in them to idleness; but in reading, in patient intelligent culture and progress, that is where I expect you need consideration, resolution and help. Do let us have a good deal of talk on this when we meet, but I must say one or two things.

First of all, I am afraid of your reading too hard, for (as I said) I do not think you are a lazy man. You have a strong will, and you rule yourself by it well, and I am afraid of your driving yourself too hard through intellectual work. I should like to speak of ourselves as in the same boat. I wish you would talk more, and write more. There is a certain mental crudeness, abruptness, almost a hardness, your thoughts being as it were wrapped up, involved too tight. This I long to see unfolded, softened, expanded. I do not know how to express what I mean, or what remedies to suggest, but I should say:—

Need of intellectual culture.
Need of deepening in spiritual love.

For the first, my own plan with myself has been never to consider myself likely to do anything in an intellectual way, but I regard reading as a duty to enable one to carry out one's vocation in dealing with the souls of men. In this way it has helped me, and it may you, to go quietly, regularly, laboriously on with intellectual work, regarding it as a means to an end, and hoping rather that God would bless one's well intentioned, well regulated efforts than expecting any great result in itself, and keep the labour of reading always by one, and to view it under the shadow of the Cross to read by the lamp of sacrifice; and that not impulsively, but in a spirit of quiet self-devotion. Do you know a book by Henri Perreyve, called *La Journée d'un Malade?* There is a beautiful chapter in it called *Courage et Travail.* Do you see, dear man, at all what I mean? I think you need to talk the question out more fully of intellectual work, and then you will be able to deal more clearly with the specific temptation and weariness in that part of your duty. But then, dearest child, I must add a word on the other head. We both need deepening more and more in divine love—in fact, real love of God and love of man in God, or God in man, makes all labour light—and, therefore, reading; and we need to be more kind, more considerate, less selfish even in carrying out religious plans, more ready to acknowledge God's Presence in others, and to fall in quietly and brightly with their different ways—freedom from any *religious harshness*, a docile, child-like, simple, loving spirit. This, dearest child, is what I long for for you, and for myself, and which I feel, through the very effort to read and work, to be in danger of missing. It is so difficult to be firm without being hard, consistent and not obstinate. The remedy, I believe, more *humility*, more love.

Now, dear man, I must stop.

Now don't read too hard, but realise it as a duty, and let us talk when we meet. I go back to Cuddesdon on Friday till Monday, and then I am going away again to my brother in Essex. His children knock me about, and do me heaps of good. I should like you to know them.

God bless you, dearest friend. Remember me in your prayers. . . . Don't be afraid of bothering me with letters. These sort of letters are my greatest pleasure.

XXV.

TO THE SAME—ON GOD'S DISCIPLINE AND GUIDANCE.

BUXTON, *July* 22, 1874.

Thank you for your second letter. It was very kind of you. The first made me anxious. I do hope you will see your way. One thing, dear friend, let me press on you, *be sure of God's love*, do not think of Him as *keeping back punishments* to stop you from future pleasures and success. That is not it. He may most likely, almost certainly, see that you require discipline, which may involve correction and suffering, on account of the past, but it will be so managed as to be rather preparation for future work, and fitness for greater blessings from Him. An abiding sorrow for sin, a readiness to take all crosses, and troubles and suffering as being what we deserve is quite right, and not inconsistent with what I mean. The truth rather is that it is difficult to get punishment enough unless one is very careful to watch the many daily, most delicate but most consistent and efficacious, means of discipline which God gives in daily life. Our pardon we must ACCEPT, we can never work out our sins' guilt by any amount of suffering. I want to get you quite clear in this, because you sometimes write as though you feared God had some punishment in reserve. Make up your mind to take anything from Him once for all, and then let the grateful love cast out the fear.

This does not mean that you should shut out the wish to lead a life of self-denial and self-devotion, above what many are called to. It only means if you feel called to it go into it in a spirit of grateful hope.

One other point, dear friend, if you will let me speak plainly. You evidently need care in checking impulses and feelings. You will get all right, I believe, but I would be careful, for this reason. I should think to continue at home work, for a time at least, would be best, and for the same reason best to continue where you are (though other reasons may alter this), and get a steady habit of self-control, so as to do the Divine Will in little daily duties—this is the inner armour of the saints—but I cannot tell what He may tell you, or where call you. That must be waited for. All I feel able to do is to suggest these preliminary thoughts which you need, I think, where-ever you may be. Do not be offended at my writing so plainly; time, perseverance, gentleness will help to make it all plain.

God bless you and guide you. . . .

XXVI.

TO THE SAME—ON HIS DECISION TO REMAIN AT HIS POST FOR THE PRESENT INSTEAD OF GOING TO ZANZIBAR.

BUXTON, *August*, 5, 1874.

Thank you for your letter. You never need fear "wearying me" if I can be any use. Your letter was a distinct relief to me, and, as far as I can see, I think you have decided rightly. I think you could probably not do more service for the Church than by staying with Mr. B. at A., and I think it will be best also for yourself to take a steady piece of work after prayerful consideration, simply from choice of the Divine Will through many conflicting impulses. This, I hope and believe, must bring its reward, and add to you right confidence, and peace, and happiness: and work from duty in a spirit of hopeful love is, perhaps, the safest and happiest state.

There are those who work from a spirit of love without any consciousness of duty, and that may be the highest state; but most of us need sometime or other the strengthening and purifying of our will under the test of duty or obedience. Only, dearest friend, don't let my hard, rough, dull words distress you. You know when I write to you I never say anything in *praise;* hence I take for granted that you know how highly I think of you, and how much I love you, but my object is to help you on to be better still, and you do need to be more free from acting from impulse and changing motives. I might fill the letter with praising you for all you have done, and say how much you are liked by everybody, and how good it is of you even to think of spending your life, or the brightest years of it, in a heathen slave market. All this I do see, and am most thankful for, but you have got to get, by God's help, to heaven yourself, as well as take others there, and, as you have asked me to help you, I feel bound always to keep sternly true, and only to try to lead you on, forgetting that which is behind. Pray do not let my letters distress you, be sure they are meant in love, and be sure they must be written in much ignorance and full of imperfection.

But I am very thankful that you have decided as you have, and done it as you have by seeking to know His Will.

There is indeed a prospect of plenty of work in England just now, under conditions which will need patience and courage.

God bless you.

XXVII.

TO THE SAME—ON DEVELOPMENT OF CHARACTER.

OXFORD, *October* 11, 1874.

You were indeed quite right, and your kind letter was an unexpected and undeserved refreshment. It was truly kind of you, and I thank you for it, but even more thankful am I if you have gained any good. I thought it was simple, and real, and I enjoyed it very *much*, especially the feeling that dear E.'s life was now telling so beautifully. His patience and self-denying watchfulness of us all were most beautiful and helpful.

I think all you say in your letter about yourself is quite right. I should not attempt so much to *undo*. Even what you feel you did beyond what was strictly right was done with a mixed intention, partly good, and I should rather trust to the untrue falling off by itself, only taking care for the future not to add to the unreal. In this I think you will, please God, gain clearness, and strength, and peace. Do not be over scrupulous at first, and expect not to be quite right at once, but if you aim at the greater simpleness of purpose, sincerity of character, I think you will find you are working in the right direction. I shall only ask you to believe how much I feel your kindness. You have often refreshed, and helped me, and I thank you very sincerely for it. To see you getting on so well is a greater pleasure to me than I can express.

God bless you and guide you. . . .

XXVIII.

TO A FRIEND—ON HIS MARRIAGE.

ROTTERDAM, *Sunday, July* 30, 1876.

This direction will a little explain to you my unaccountable silence! I got your letter just before I started on the 1st of July, and I have been meaning to write ever since, and now your second letter has reached me. What shall I say? First, forgive me! and then, may God indeed bless you! Dearest friend, Christian marriage is to me one of the greatest mysteries with which we have to do, and most sincerely do I wish you *both* all the mysterious fulness of the blessing of the many mysteries into which you enter; and for your own character, dear friend, I think it will be just what you want to save you, I trust, from that wretched selfish hardness into which I am conscious in my single life to have fallen. You must be very happy, dear friend. I can conceive no earthly happiness greater than to be given by God the whole of the earthly, nay, more than earthly, the whole of the human love of another. This is one of God's greatest gifts, one of the closest symbols of what He is, and of the union between Himself and us. May you richly enjoy this great gift, and may it enlarge the power of your love, and help you to turn with yet a larger heart to *His*, and *Him*. It must be a great *rest* for you. It ought to give you a good lift clean away from vanity and care of what others think, knowing you have not the thoughts, but the *love* of *one*, and you can tell her that her religious business is to love her husband and yours to love *her*. That is wonderful! And then, if it should please God, to give you yet another mystery, and give you children! This adding to the number of eternal beings is more than any angel or archangel is allowed to do. Great are the mysteries, dear friend, into which you are entering. May He Who only knows so guide you both that you may fulfil all His mind.

As to marrying you, the only difficulty is my residence. I am bound hand and foot from August 25th to September 15th, and in the *Long* [Vacation] it is difficult to get a substitute. Still, if I can, I will; and also I hear a rumour about cleaning the cathedral. All this I shall know when I get back, and I will write again.

Now, good-bye. I shall be so glad to think of you settled and free from all those vanities and selfish hardnesses, which, alas! I know too well too often make up the character of the so-called harder single life. It need not be so I know, but too many of us, when alone, live with self and worse, and the presence of another would help to drive all that self and worse away. To have the presence of another regenerate person given to one is indeed another Sacrament of grace, a new way of being with Him.

God bless you a thousand times, dearest friend, and lift you far away above all that I can ever say or think, and help you with a new and renewed power to tell the people that He is Love. . . .

XXIX.

TO A FATHER—ON THE BIRTH OF HIS FIRST CHILD.

OXFORD, *S. Stephen's* [*Day*], 1877.

I am so glad. Thank you so much for letting me share your joy so quickly. It is indeed a wonderful gift, and must be the letting loose of new floods of love. Love, I believe, *descends*. Parents love their children more than children can their parents, so that children can only enter into the fulness of the parents' love by becoming parents themselves. This is a wonderful true law, running down to the love which animals have for their young, and then running up to the endless, unchangeable ineffable knowledge—surpassing love of our Father which is in heaven. So, dearest friend, this should give you a new glimpse into the love which has taught you from your youth up. Pardon all this sermon, but it is nice to keep finding out fresh proofs of the unexpected love which is waiting for us descending and ascending, and ready always to descend.

Dearest friend, if I can come I will, but we go to St. Leonards on Monday for a fortnight, and my good mother says you ought not to have your little one christened for a *month*, and begs your good wife will be careful not to catch cold. She sends her *kindest congratulations* and best wishes, so does J.; but let me hear nearer the time, and if I can I will run up and back for the great mystery. Now, good-bye. Give my kindest rejoicings to your dear wife, and may He Who has given, yet give beyond what you ask and think.

God bless you. . . .

XXX.

TO A PRIEST—ON DIFFICULTIES IN A COUNTRY PARISH.

LEIGH, ESSEX, *January* 19, 1871.

How good of you to be so good natured when I have been so neglectful, and, after all, I think I had better say nothing. So much depends on the small circumstances of the case and place, which only one near can know, so I really think the best advice I can give is to refer you to Mr. H., whose judgment would, I should think, be good. For the rest I should try and win the hearts of the servants and poor, and so make *them* my champions. If they found good and comfort from the catechising I expect it would soon get round to the ears of my lord and lady, and they would come. Win them by touching their hearts. Try and think what THEY want in their spiritual life, not merely what *you* want to tell them. The poor, and many others, are mostly right in their *heads*; they go wrong in their *affections* and in their *wills*, and we must go after them where they go, and meet them where they are wandering, preaching to them in sermons full of *love*, and showing them how to get power and strengthen their *wills*. In this way we must come to them in parables and human ways, and attracting them to us by the human side, leading them on to the divine. This is, I believe, the principle of the Incarnation. Man would not look up to God, so God came down to man, and walked before him, and with him, and attended him in his daily life, that leading him to Himself He might in the end carry him up to God. See, dear person, we must come down, and be very simple and kind, and help them where they need help. So you will win them, and as they find you winning their souls to God, so they will find their true *peace*, and they will soon tell the great people by their own transformation what good there is in the services of the Church. Good-bye. This is no good, I fear. God bless you and help you to win them back to the Divine.

XXXI.

TO A PRIEST—ON CHANGE OF WORK.

OXFORD, *August* 3, 1877.

Pardon my delay. I am very sorry to see that you are not settled, as I had hoped in work that suited you.

I am sorry I do not know anyone with whom you could exchange, but I will not forget your wish. I will most gladly help you if I can.

May I venture to ask whether you have considered finally the necessity for change? If you are free to teach, and the money arrangements are sufficient, I should really question whether you were not providentially in your right place. One often does most when one is not most aware of it. *I* should not choose the University to work in if I had my choice. I would rather be with the simplest agricultural poor, but it is not so arranged. Do write to me again, and say if you really must change on grounds of doctrine or finance. I think you would do the rich a deal of good.

God guide you, dear friend, and bless you. . . .

XXXII.

TO ONE OF HIS YOUNGER CLERGY WHO HAD ENTERED ON A NEW SPHERE OF WORK.

January 5, 1895.

Thank you so much for writing, and for sending me the card and verses of dear old Canon A. Please give him my kindest remembrances.

I am very glad you are so happy, and I hope the experience will be just what you want. It is wonderful what can be done if only we go the right way. Nothing is so beautiful as the beauty of good people; it is most refreshing. I long to see it brought out in the country villages. I believe it might be done with God's help, if people only would not run away from one diocese to another! That, you see, is my jealous condition of mind! No, I am really glad you are where you are, because I hope it will enable you to work all the better somewhere hereafter.

God bless you and keep you.

Believe me always,

Yours most affectionately.

XXXIII.

TO THE SAME.

1895.

Your letter was a great help and comfort to me. It was very good of you to write.

As one gets older it is a great help and encouragement if any who are beginning life can make any use of one in any way. You may reckon on my love whenever you want it.

I should always be glad to see you, if you think it would refresh you in any way.

God bless you and keep you.

XXXIV.

TO A PRIEST—ON LEAVING HIS DIOCESE.

November 29, 1901.

How can I at all thank you for your loving letter? I am sincerely sorry to lose you from my diocese, both for my own sake, and for the sake of my people, for I always felt that you would love them in the highest and best way. You have done this, I know, as far as you could in your small parish. I am sorry you must leave them, but I trust you are quite right, and do so under the clear order of the doctor, for he is God's voice for us in matters of health. I wish I could have done more for you. Indeed, I feel I have been useless to you, except so far as you say you have been able to get good for yourself. One of the hard parts of a Bishop's life is the distance he has to be from individuals; especially the poor. I often long to stop in a village after a Confirmation, and see each one separately, but one comes and goes, and we don't meet again! I know for myself it is a most merciful and providential discipline. In a parish I should be too much absorbed in individuals; but it is hard to keep loving without some little response, and so, dearest brother, your letter is a real comfort and help to me, and I will try and keep on, and do better, and love my dear people more and more, even though I never hear of their love as you have so kindly let me hear from you. We need truth and love. S. John's Gospel is full of *both* words, truth and love. The truth, the faith in its true proportion. This keeps us steady, and enables us to open and guide the minds, as well as the hearts of the people.

If ever you would like to come to us for a few days' rest believe me you will always be welcome. I have written to the Bishop of Winton about you. God bless you and your dear wife and children, and guide you and make you a true guide and blessing to them.

XXXV.

TO THE SAME—IN HIS NEW (AND MORE SOUTHERLY) PARISH.

September 9, 1902.

Pardon my delay in thanking you for your most kind letter, far too kind, dear friend, but very comforting. Old age is apt to be depressing and to make us feel useless, and a kind word of love cheers up an old Bishop as well as a young child. I am afraid I must not do what you so kindly want; my work will be pretty constant as soon as I get back. But some day, if I may, I should love to come and see you all again. Why not come to us for the Retreat? It begins on Monday, September 22nd, and ends on the 26th. I will keep a room for you in case you can come. It will do you good, and do us good to have you with us again.

I hope you are keeping well, and Mrs. M. and the children. Everybody says the south people are much more difficult to rouse in matters of religion than the northern. But in time, please God, you will win them. You must go half steam, but with the full power of your love. They are shy, and meek, and afraid. Like fishing in the clear slow chalk streams of Hampshire, it requires very fine tackle and a delicate hand! God bless you, dearest friend, and guide you. My love and blessing to you all. Always your loving.

XXXVI.

TO THE SAME—ON LOVE OF SOULS.

January 22, 1904.

How can I possibly thank you for all your goodness to me and mine? Thank you indeed for your kind gift to our Grimsby Fund. It shall be entered on the list of donations as you wish. It is most generous and good of you. I thank you too for the most attractive looking gift more directly for myself. I have sometimes thought what an interesting book might be written by such a treatment of the Psalms, but I did not know it had been done.[1] I shall look forward with great delight to reading it. I have already dipped into it, and I think it will help me with my Lent letters on the Bible. And for all your kind words I cannot attempt to thank you, dear friend, but they are a great comfort to me, not because I deserve them (I know that), but because they convey the inestimable comfort of responsive love. At Wheatley and Cuddesdon and Oxford I enjoyed through God's unspeakable goodness such abundance of love, that the more formal life of a Bishop, I fear, does make me cold, and hard, and selfish. You, dear friend, have helped to keep alive the earlier and simpler life of love —that is the end of life. Do come again whenever you like, and forgive the little attention that I showed you. Please thank your dear wife and the dear

[1] Prothero—"*The Psalms in Human Life,*" which his corresponden had sent to the Bishop.

children for their kind Christmas gift. Accept my love and blessing to you all.

XXXVII.

TO ONE OF HIS CHAPLAINS—CONFIRMATIONS.

July, 1891.

I am in a mess! But I must write a line to thank you for yours.

I began at 4.30 this morning, and made a wretched sermon at B., where we went last evening, and we have had a long, but lovely, day. Quite ideal, if I was only fit for it. Do pray with all your might for better Bishops. These people might be angels and archangels straight off, if we were only decent! It is most sad.

XXXVIII.

ON APPOINTING ONE OF HIS CLERGY TO A BENEFICE.

April 29, 1895.

I did not know till your Vicar told me of your own sorrow. May God comfort you all. I know how much the tearing up of the old home love tries one.

Pardon me if I go on at once to another matter, which I can hardly keep from you. You will probably have heard that your good Vicar has most nobly undertaken the work at C. for me. Now I want to ask you if you will take charge of S. John's in his place? You know the work, and you are known there, and, I think, with God's help, you might add to what you have already done by taking charge of the parish. It will be a new and great responsibility, but one which, with God's help, I believe you will be able to bear.

You will, of course, find new demands on your own personal judgment, but that only means that the time has come for you to make the offering of yourself to God in His Church complete, and to do the *bit* of work He has prepared you for. May God guide and bless you in your decision.

XXXIX.

TO AN OLD FRIEND—PAROCHIAL WORK.

LINCOLN, *December* 31, 1901.

Ah! those Cuddesdon days were very wonderful! I fear I have fallen below the high aims and hopes we had then. It is hard sometimes when people go wrong; but thank God I believe in the people, and love them down to the ground. I am never happier than when I go to our little country parishes and talk to the dear things.

God bless you, dear friend, and make you a blessing to others.

Always your most sincere and affectionate.

XL.

TO A PRIEST—IN SORROW.

LINCOLN, *January* 28, 1908.

Pardon the delay in thanking you for your most kind letter for my birthday. It is very good of you to remember one still. As long as you can, don't forget me in your prayers. I need them more and more as strength declines.

I am sorry your good son is going out of my diocese, but I am glad he is married and that he has a home of his own. I trust he will be happy.

I was very sorry to hear how much sorrow and trial you have had, and still have. We cannot understand the mystery of sorrow. We can "see Jesus," the "Man of Sorrows," and see how His earthly ministry apparently was a failure. They did not care for Him—wonderful and purifying example for us all, warning us against the dangers of popularity and apparent success. May we keep the seed of the Word pure, and keep following His example. If you will send me a postcard in about *ten* days I will send you a copy of my Charge. Perhaps some of it you might like.

God bless you, dear brother, and your family and parish. . . .

XLI.

TO ONE OF HIS CLERGY—ON HIS ACCEPTING A BENEFICE.

January 16, 1909.

Thank you very much. I am very glad and thankfull that you have felt able to accept C. It is a comfort to me, for I hope that, after so many years of hard work, you will be more comfortably placed, and yet there is full and interesting work to do. I shall be anxious to find a successor for S. John's, but I shall have your prayers, I am sure. May God bless and guide your work for the Church in this diocese for many years to come, if it be His Will.

I shall be anxious to know how the house difficulty works out. You had better look at B.'s house; but I feel pretty sure that the stabling and gardens there are all too large.

XLII.

TO A PRIEST WORKING IN THE COLONIES—RITUAL TROUBLES.

SWITZERLAND, *August* 27, 1898.

I have often wished for half-an-hour to write to you, and now, being here on my holiday, I can get it.

How are you getting on? I hear of you from time to time from H., and he always reports of you all as "well."

I daresay you have seen in the papers all about the ritual troubles. I hope they will be overruled for good. Some men had been adopting all kinds of mediæval and modern Roman ways, for which there is really no sort of authority in the Church of England, or in the Primitive Church. Now, I hope we shall come back nearer to the true English position of Holy Scripture and the Primitive Church. We need not be surprised if the zeal of some young men carried them too far in the matter of Confession and Eucharistic doctrine.

I believe most of them will be willing to come back to the Church of England standard, and the young ones who are coming up can have the danger made plain to them. One loves the zeal and self-devotion of many of the men who have been led on too far; but some, I fear, are in danger of losing sight of the highest and most spiritual things, and becoming humanly ecclesiastical. I hope in a little time all will settle down, and be better than before, because nearer the truth.

God bless you, dear B., and your wife and children. Let me hear from you again before long. . . .

XLIII.

ON CONFESSION.

LEIGH, ROCHFORD, *January* 15, 1869.

I am sorry that, being from home, your letter has not reached me till this morning, and, therefore (unless, as I hope, Mr. D. may have told you of my absence), you will not have been saved the trouble of going to Cuddesdon to-day. I hope to return on the 22nd, and I shall be very glad to see you any day (except Monday, the 25th) you name. Perhaps I can then explain to you some of the points in your former letter. On the power of absolution you would find Bishop Andrewes' sermons on "The Power of the Keys" very valuable. I think they are in Volume V. of his works.

I would recommend you to come over if you please, and talk over these points of difficulty, and to get them, so far as may be, settled, and then you will be more able to prepare yourself in Lent, as you proposed. Do not be surprised at finding difficulties. At first it almost must be so, but, by degrees, please God, you will see your way quietly and firmly.

God help and bless you.

P.S.—I may add some short answers to the questions.

It is not possible to mention each instance of sin, it is enough to mention the *kind* of sin and number, and the chief instances that indicate the degree :—

(*a*) Kind;
(*b*) Frequency;
(*c*) Degree.

Confession does not imply penance necessarily.

Penance does not imply abstaining from Holy Communion necessarily.

See Bishop Andrewes.

See clearly, and resolve by God's help to devote whatever fragments of broken health you may have, just as thoroughly as you would devote a whole strong unbroken life.

Heads of self-examination :—

(1) Deeds.
(2) Words.
(3) Thoughts.

Tendency of my character through *not* reaching to any *outward* or *inward* act.

XLIV.

TO A PRIEST—ON HEARING CONFESSIONS.

CHRIST CHURCH, *April* 12, 1880.

As a first and general rule I should decline to hear the confession of young girls without the leave of their parents. Generally speaking, either the parents give leave after they are convinced of the sincerity of their child's distress, or the distress is found to be one that need not hinder the child from communicating with a quiet conscience. When young people are confirmed to a great extent the parents admit by the act that their children have reached years of discretion, and, therefore, may judge for themselves.

But still, as confession is regarded more or less as an *extraordinary* act, it is hardly honest to assume that it is permitted unless definitely allowed. I do, therefore, desire even confirmed young women to get leave from their parents, at least as long as they may be reasonably supposed to be living under their parents' guidance.

If, AFTER INSTRUCTION, a young person feels unable to communicate without confession, and yet cannot get her parents' leave, I should receive such a one to confession. I should let this be known as your general practice.

With regard to the Sisters, I would not let them interfere with my own rules, but, if they think differently, let them make known their opinion and practice, and then, if thoroughly understood, you might receive those sent to you by the Sisters, it being understood that in placing the child under the Sisters' influence the parents left its future treatment to their discretion.

Of course, all general rules need equitable adjustment, but a clear open line of conduct is far better than suspicion.

God bless you and guide you.

XLV.

TO A PRIEST—ON CONFESSION.

CHRIST CHURCH, OXFORD, *June* 19, 1883.

Your letter needs no apology. If I can help you I shall be thankful.

It is not easy to explain many of our religious acts so as to be satisfactory simply to the logical faculty. It may seem unreasonable to have an absolution in the daily office, and in the Holy Communion, and to repeat the Lord's Prayer, asking for forgiveness, so frequently in one Sunday morning service; and yet when the moral and spiritual side of our nature is appealed to, these acts and prayers are found to have a real place, and to be not contradictory to our reason.

With regard to the particular matter about which you ask, the following is the line of thought which has seemed to me most loyal to our Prayer Book, and most satisfactory to people's needs:—

(1) Confession to a priest is not necessary, God will pardon on true repentance; therefore confession of our sins to God, with true sorrow and purpose of amendment, and prayer for pardon through Christ, will bring pardon.

The necessity of confession to a priest once a year was not enforced till the Council of Lateran (1215 A.D.).

Dr. Pusey has a long note on this in his

volume of Tertullian in the Library of the Fathers; Notes L. and M.

(2) Our Prayer Book says, as you know, in the exhortation to Holy Communion, that if a person cannot find peace in this way, then their duty is to go to the priest for confession.

We should, I think, teach people this, and trust to the Holy Spirit to guide them when to come.

(3) In the case of sickness, as you know, we are to move the sick person to make a special confession if there is any weighty matter.

Here again, if we all did this, I think a great number would be able to see what they ought to do, without any great difficulty.

(4) If you look at S. Augustine *De Symbolo*, section 18, *Remissionem Peccatorum*, you will see that he speaks of *three* ways in which sins are forgiven, "Ergo tribus modis dimittuntur peccata in Ecclesiâ, in *Baptismate, in Oratione, in humilitate majori penitentiæ*." S. Augustine considered prayer, *i.e.*, the Lord's Prayer, to be sufficient for cleansing the daily faults: "Ad haec (levia peccata) quotidiana oratio delenda sufficeret." The graver sins (adulteria aut aliqua facta immania) he would expect good Christians to keep free from (nolite illa committere).

If you look in S. Augustine's *Sermones ad Competentes* (57, 58 Bened. ed.) you will see the sort of sins he calls "*levia*," and which would be covered by the Lord's Prayer. We ought, perhaps, to remember that S. Augustine was speaking very much to people preparing for Baptism as *adults*, and, therefore, they would start with their eyes more open than some of us did. However, it comes, I think, to this:—

(*a*) Our Church does not make confession to a priest necessary.

(*b*) She instructs her children to guide themselves with God's help, by God's law, if they can; if they want help then to come to a priest.

(*c*) In sickness our Church urges confession to a priest, if there has been weighty cause.

(*d*) The Church of England bids her clergy teach what Holy Scripture teaches, and what the Fathers have gathered out of the same.

S. Augustine and others would say, Try and live on with only such daily faults as the Lord's Prayer will cover, but if you have fallen into the greater sins then you had better get the help of the priest through confession and absolution.

I know that many good people use confession who have not fallen into the greater acts of sin, but who have sinned in will, and, if they are real in such use of it, I think our Church allows it, and S. Cyprian and S. Gregory the Great speak of sins of thought, and

Origen speaks of going to a priest in matters which are doubtful; but, on the whole, if we keep to the general line of our Church's teaching, I think the rest will be made clear to us as we want it.

I venture to send you a letter I was obliged once to print, but do not read more of it than you like. The references may help you.[1]

If I can help you any more I shall be very glad to do so.

May God guide you and bless you, and make you a guide and blessing to others.

[1] *Letter to Rev. C. J. Elliott*, published by Parker, Oxford.

XLVI.

TO A MISSIONARY BISHOP—ON CONFESSION.

MÜRREN, *August* 18, 1905.

Pardon my not making time to write to you, and thank you for your two kind letters; but you know how difficult it is for a bishop to be good!

I am here on my holidays with F. and R. The former sends his respectful love; the latter would if he dared. They are a great help and joy to me.

In answer to your two letters, I fear it was partly my fault in being too secularly cheerful, and so not helping you as I might have done in higher things. Indeed, in those ways it often occurs to me that I was more use as Canon King than E. Lincoln. But, I suppose, if, as we trust, we are working with, and for God, then we may expect not to see exactly what we are doing, because the plan is His, and we only see a little part of it.

As to confession by letter, I have heard of it, but never adopted it. I should venture to recommend waiting till you can get to New York, or till some Bishop comes, or Cowley Father.

I have not seen Bishop Churton's book, though I think I saw a notice of it in the *Guardian*. The experience of my life would lead me to look most to God's individual care and discipline of our souls. Of course I go to confession still. But God's discipline seems to me most wonderful and awful, as well as most merciful in its adaptation to our real needs, and the real needs of our character.

Have you seen Illingworth's last book, *Christian Character?* It is excellent, showing that the real aim is the union of one's whole personality—will, reason, affections, body—with God.

If I live, come and see us again. That God may guide, and support, and bless you is the sincere prayer of your most sincere and affectionate.

XLVII.

TO A CANDIDATE FOR ORDINATION.

CUDDESDON VICARAGE, WHEATLEY,
October 6, 1871.

Thank you for your letter. I am sorry you have not been well, and that you have had so much anxiety in your family, and on your own account.

I hope you have done nothing but what will turn out well in the end.

I do not know P. or Mr. T., but I will hope that it is all well. If, when you go down to see the place you find anything that seriously makes you doubt, I will gladly give you my advice if you will kindly tell me what the point is, and, if it is necessary (which we need but suppose), I should think Mr. T. would release you from your engagement. With this possibility of liberty I should be quite at rest, and wait to see the place. I shall hope that you will then see no reason for altering your decision.

Regarding yourself :—

(1) I would recommend you to begin, and say daily the *Veni Creator*.

(2) To set apart half-an-hour, if you can, for meditative reading, such as the *Memoriale Vitæ Sacerdotalis*; or Heygate's *Ember Hours*, or his *Good Shepherd*; or Dr. Pusey's *Commentaries on Hosea* or *Jonah* might be well used with reference to your Ordination.

(3) I should recommend you to go to confession before your Ordination. If you are not coming this way I could advise you to go to some priest elsewhere. I may be in London in Advent for a night, and would gladly see you then.

That God may guide and bless you in your preparation for His great service is my sincere prayer. . . .

XLVIII.

ON DAILY COMMUNION.

CUDDESDON, *August* 25, 1860.

Many thanks for your letter.

With regard to daily Communion. I am not able to find out from history that it was ever the general practice of the whole Church. All I can find out is this:—

In the Acts of the Apostles it is probable there was daily Communion; but observe, it was in connection with the Apostles themselves, and, perhaps, would not prove more than that the clergy [should] offer any nearest to them the opportunity.

For the first eight hundred years daily Communion did exist in some places, but was not the general custom.

Early in the fifth century the great Augustine was asked his opinion on the point, and he said that he thought weekly Communion ought to be the general thing; but, more than that, he would leave to the consciences of his people. He compared those who wished for daily Communion to Zacchæus, who received our LORD *gladly*, and those who feared more than weekly, to the Centurion, who would not ask Christ to come under his roof. Both these, he adds, did receive Christ.

Hence I do not find that the mass of Christian people were ever daily communicants (except, perhaps, at the very first).

My own opinion is that I am not able to attempt daily Communion myself; but, if it please God to spare me, I think, as a priest, I ought to be able, and, most likely, by God's help, I shall do so.[1]

For yourself I should be quite happy if you and all the laity were weekly communicants. Still, if we end our days together I believe you might be just as much and more fit for daily Communion than myself; hence I would press it upon no one, but allow it to any, specially the clergy.

God bless you, my dearest Charlie. Give my best love to dear old father and mother, and your sister.

I am still on my back, but much better—really quite well.

[1] When he became Bishop, he always had a daily Celebration in his Chapel, and nearly always was himself the Celebrant.

XLIX.

TO A PRIEST IN WEAK HEALTH IN CHARGE OF A HOSPITAL—ON FASTING.

CHRIST CHURCH, OXFORD, *August* 21, 1877.

Thanks for your note. Certainly eat meat whenever you feel you want it.

And for the first six months I shall advise you to eat meat *every day*, Fridays and all. After that you could, perhaps, tell better how you could manage. If two fasts come together I should still certainly eat meat on one of them (*i.e.*, after the *six* months). After six months you might find that you could make a difference if the work is lighter in the hospital. If on any particular Friday you felt not to need it, then be ready to go without it.

But for six months EAT.

God bless you and preserve you. You are doing good to us outside, besides your patients.

L.

TO A LADY—ON TROUBLES.

CHRIST CHURCH, OXFORD,
St. Peter's Day, 1876.

I have been so unsettled in my movements that I could not answer your letter before, and now I go away to-morrow till August 10th (about). I hope you will be able to get on. Take the daily troubles as the very best discipline you could possibly have. They are simply God's own words to you. He sees what you want. Bear the daily work patiently, and try to make the Church your comfort and resting place. Don't be surprised or disappointed if you are not always bright and happy; such blessings are indeed most precious, but not necessary, and brighter days may very likely come quite as soon as you are ready for them.

God help you and bless you.

LI.

TO THE SAME—ON ASKING FORGIVENESS.

CHRIST CHURCH, *November* 6, 1877.

I am sorry to hear of your anxiety, but these troubles which come to us, and are not brought by ourselves, come freed of half their weight. We can trust them that they are for our good. With regard to your question, I do not, perhaps, know exactly all the circumstances, so that I may be more or less advising in the dark; but, as far as I can see, I should recommend you to ask forgiveness from your mother while you can, not because I have any doubt about your being forgiven, but such a course is the most natural. Almost all people, more or less, would do so; for all in different degrees must be conscious of imperfectly rendered duties; so that there would be nothing strange in your doing so, and I think it is the safest course to take. You might regret not having done so when too late. For yourself, too, it would probably be the best thing to do. If you are conscious of some degree of failure there will be some little amends. So I should advise you simply to ask God's help and guidance to do it. I must add very sincere congratulations, and good wishes, on the help and hope of happiness which God has so lovingly granted you.

God bless you. . . .

LII.

TO A LADY WHO WAS DEPRESSED BECAUSE SHE WAS NOT MAKING PROGRESS.

August 23, 1881.

Pardon my delay. I do not know any book definitely to meet the case you ask about. But in Keble's *Spiritual Letters* there are some which would be very applicable. I should recommend that book, if your friend has not got it. Like all K.'s writing, it is so gentle and so strong, so clear and so deep, so high and so well balanced. Any of the volumes of his sermons, too, would be sure to be useful, and give your friend a steady and hopeful mind. Hope is a duty, and brightness, inward if not outward—more or less—should go with it. I delight in Ezekiel, with the rainbow round about, and the brightness. He is the prophet of hope.

I hope you are well, and your brother. My love to him, and to you.

God bless you and take care of you.

LIII.

TO A PRIEST—A MORAL CASE.

CUDDESDON VICARAGE, *October* 19, 1868.

My first pleasure in writing is to disappoint you in being able to say, like other wicked people, "he never writes." You see, dear man, the horrid injustice which men of real businesslike habits are liable to, from an envious and ignorant public!

I was very glad to hear you were at work, and on the whole satisfactorily.

The drunkard I should have loved more if he had not had his pocket picked, or, rather, if he had not wished it to be filled. Still, you must love him for all that. It requires experience to know people. It is better to be over charitable than over strict. I am sure we must run the risk of the charge brought against our Lord of being too easy with sinners. It is a great difficulty, but that is the line, I am sure. I should try and get the poor man to take up really a life of self-discipline. Probably he lives on the chance all the year, and then *breaks* out. If he would aim at doing anything as a duty, at times when not tempted to break out he would be gaining the habit of self-control, which would be ready made when the temptation to break out came. He is probably *careless* as a habit. It is not possible often to conquer one's sins, unless one cuts away *all*, then each goes.

He is probably sulky, selfish, swears, lazy, proud, conceited, and has fifty other faults. Cut them off, and he will see that being once better he is better able to go on.

Never mind being weary of visiting, *go on.* It is very wearying and unsatisfactory at the time, but it tells in the end, and contributes to their confidence in you.

God keep you, dear D. Your sympathy and appreciation of Christian refinement were a great comfort to me. Good-bye. Remember me in your prayers. . . .

LIV.

TO A PRIEST—A MORAL CASE.

OLD PALACE, LINCOLN, *February* 12, 1901.

It is very sad. I hope to write a letter to you all shortly; but it can only be by slow degrees, and the gradual raising of public opinion that we can hope for improvement.

I think you acted quite rightly in burying, and entering the names of the poor children.

The queston of marriage is more difficult:—

(1) Being so young, they may hardly know their own minds, or whether there is fair probability that their characters would suit one another. If there seems to be fair prospect of their suiting one another—as from stations of life, dispositions, etc., and as far as you can tell a real attachment beyond mere passing animal passion—if they show any penitence, and willingness to wait and suffer for their sin, then I should incline to their marrying. If there is none of this, but rather bitterness and mutual recrimination, I should not advise marriage, but leave them alone (except so far as trying to bring them to repentance).

(2) Where they should be married is also difficult. I think it depends chiefly on the effect on others in the parish. If we could use full discipline and feel sure of their penitence,

> after confession and absolution, they might (after a year, say) be admitted to Holy Communion, and then be married in church (the difference between the first and second Epistle to the Corinthians is less than a year, I believe).

Short of this, I think it must turn (1) on their own penitence; (2) on the effect on the parish. If their general reputations had been good, and their families good, and you could hope well of their future, I should incline to marrying them, as quietly as possible, without bells, in the church. If you think it would be a scandal to the parish, I should advise the registry office, and try and do my best to bring them in due time to Holy Communion.

It is very sad. May God have mercy upon us and help us.

LV.

TO A NURSE IN THE DIOCESE OF BLOEMFONTEIN.

CHRIST CHURCH, OXFORD, *July* 10, 1880.

I hope you will forgive my sad delay in thanking you for your letter of December 20th, 1879. It is not that I have forgotten you, but my life is a busy and interrupted one. I have never learnt to work in a steady businesslike way; so many things are left undone. It is very difficult to keep a bright free spirit with much business routine, but I hope to do better. I was so sorry to hear that you had been so ill; but, thank God, I hope you are by this time well and strong again, and able to nurse others. I am not surprised that you found the work at first a little disappointing, but I hope before this you have been able to see that the thing to do in life is to add to the real steady work of the building as it is really rising all round, and not to build up a perfect little tower of one's own. Probably your very power is your weakness. I mean the scientific conception which you have of nursing makes you distressed at the disorderly haphazard, rough and ready kind of way in which it must, much of it, be done.

I should think your best way would be to watch all this, and get as many *bits* as possible into proper shape and order for some future scientific combination, but to be content to say, like David: "I have *prepared* with all my might for the house of my God."

He gathered materials, but never saw them put together, or the building rise from the ground.

Some day probably God will give you one who will catch the scientific fire from you, and the torch will be handed on; all things need patience and humility, but these are the flowers, and fruit, and beauty of scientific life. It is hard and hideous without them, so I am glad to think that you are really receiving just the *double* training that is best for your real perfection.

I hope you have got to know the good Bishop well.[1] He is one of the ablest and best men I have ever known. He has a noble mind and heart, but he chafes at little things. Please give him my most respectful but sincere love, if he is near you.

Let me hear from you when you can. Your life is valuable to us here as an evidence of faith in a world beyond. Thus you are all helping us at home more than you can tell. Keep bravely, cheerfully on, for you have a blessed life before you. Let all your scientific schemes and dreams be knocked about and smashed up continually, yet keep steadily contemplating the organised perfection of your work so it will be really suited to the place and people, and be a real living organism, and not a mere imported *patch* for the poor natives and colonials to stare at.

Now, good-bye. God bless you, and guide you, and uphold you, and give you a humble and a brave victorious spirit.

[1] Bishop Webb.

LVI.

TO A YOUNG LADY—THANKS FOR AN ALTAR FRONTAL.

LINCOLN, *Epiphany*, 1892.

It would be, I think, almost the whole truth if I were to say that the greatness of the gift has been the true cause of my delay in thanking you. No doubt there has been some sloth, or shrinking from effort, but that which made the effort necessary was not carelessness, but a most real and serious appreciation of what you have done.

I do not know where I have seen any work more pleasingly beautiful than the altar frontal which you have sent me.

Where harmony in colouring is really good, it is a very real and restful pleasure to those who are capable of seeing it. We know how abundantly this is provided for in nature, but in art it often fails. In your work you appear to me to have succeeded wonderfully.

I am, therefore, truly grateful to you for the magnificence and beauty of the gift which you have been so good as to send me.

But this is not really all, or the greater part of that which caused this reply to your letter to be an effort such as I have mentioned.

This gift represents, I know, the kindness of many hearts.

When I looked over the long list of names which

you had so carefully written out for me I felt moved and ashamed, more than I can say, to think God should have given me such an abundance of love. This is wonderful enough to make one silent, except in prayer.

But even this is not all; for, indeed, the greatest ground of thankfulness has yet to be expressed. It is that you have done all this to me as His servant. It is a gift not so much to me as to my office; that is, to your Bishop as the servant of Jesus Christ sent to watch over you in this diocese. It is for His altar that you have worked this beautiful frontal, and *there*, please God, I will remember you. I can only add may God bless you all for your kindness to His servant. . . .

LVII.

TO A FRIEND—ON THE ILLNESS OF HIS SON, WHO WAS A CANDIDATE FOR ORDINATION.

April 17, 1904.

I am so very sorry to hear from the Principal of Cuddesdon that your dear son is so unwell and unable to undertake his examination this week. The Principal asks if he might do the papers in a month's time, when I hope he may be well again. If he is well enough he may certainly do this; either coming here or having his papers at Cuddesdon. Then he could be ordained at Trinity. Failing this, he might *possibly* be able to do the papers later on, and be ordained in September at Ely. I think there will be another wanting Letters Dimissory, and I could ask Ely if he would ordain them for me.

I hope, however, he may be able to do the papers in a month's time. I am so very sorry for him, and for you, dear friend. How hard it is to hold up under the different trials that come upon one! But no doubt all is ordered for the best, as we shall one day see, please God. God bless you, dear friend, and your son. . . .

LVIII.

TO A PRIEST—THE ATHANASIAN CREED.

LINCOLN, *July* 26, 1904.

It was very nice to hear of you again, though I am sorry you are so distressed. Whatever the committee may suggest with regard to the Athanasian Creed I hope nothing will be done till after the next Lambeth Conference, as we are bound up together at least with the Church in South Africa, etc.

Meanwhile, there will be time for people to express their minds and wishes. Many people, I suppose, would hesitate if we were proposing for the first time to require the creed as it stands to be recited in the public service on great festivals. Such an order was, I believe, a new departure when we made it in the reformed Prayer Book. And also it may be said that the use of the minatory clauses is not in analogy with the use of the anathemas connected with the other creeds.

At the same time I voted against any alteration at the present time. I fear it would do harm and make people think that we might yield in essentials.

The real question for people to ask themselves is: "Is *any* faith necessary?" That is really what the minatory clauses come to.

Do not be more distressed than you can help, dear friend. God will take care of His truth. We must do our bit in our day, and trust the future to His everlasting power and love.

I hope we shall meet at Cuddesdon; with my love and blessing. . . .

LIX.

TO AN OLD FRIEND—OLD AGE.

LINCOLN, *June* 27, 1905.

Thank you so much for your most kind and sympathetic letter. I quite know what you mean, and your own letter gives the true answer, "The desire for something that the world cannot give." We must look "up" and "on" rather than back for real satisfaction! Have you seen Evans' sermon[1] on dear Bishop Woodford as founder of Ely College? If not, write and make him send you a copy. It is beautiful and excellent, and rekindles old warmths of love, but that ends with looking forwards. "The natural evening is the spiritual morning."

We must not mind, but rather be thankful for the disappointments and dissatisfactions which years bring to us. It is God's way of cutting the lesser strings that tie us to the life below. It will be easier for us when we get to the end. It is not so easy as I thought it would be to keep bright, and cheerful, and

[1] Sermon by Rev. Canon A. R. Evans, who was Chaplain to Bishop Woodford throughout his Episcopate. Printed by G. H. Tyndall, Ely.

full of hope as one gets old. One saw it all in my dear mother, and in one's folly one thought one would do as well, but I see now how wonderful she was, and what a failure I am.

You must come and see us again. Are you going to Switzerland? I hope we shall get away for a month or so early in August.

Good-bye, dearest friend, "Better to have loved and lost than never to have loved at all."

Cuddesdon days do make one sad sometimes, but they were, *and are*, full of hope for better things to come.

With my love and blessing. . . .

LX.

TO A YOUNG MAN—ON THE PRESENCE OF GOD.

LINCOLN, *February* 21, 1889.

I thank you for your letter.

I am not surprised at the trouble which you experience, but I hope you will see your way before long. It is not necessary to be always thinking *directly* of God. Indeed, it is not possible. Sometimes, of course, we ought to, and can, do this, but at other times we must give our minds to what we are doing, even if it is playing and amusement. We may, of course, commit the chief periods of our time and of our occupation to God by a short ejaculatory prayer, as we do before and after meals, and before reading the Bible. So also before any study, and after any study, and such a word of prayer to bless our games that they may be innocent and refreshing to us, and to those with whom we play. In this way we can carry out the words "I have set God always before me," and adopt the motto, *Laborare est orare.*

Ejaculatory prayer is also possible during work and play, but in the main you should be satisfied with commending your work or play to God, and then throw yourself into it heartily. Write again when you like.

God bless you, and guide you, and comfort you. . . .

LXI.

ON PRESBYTERIANS WISHING FOR COMMUNION.

1909.

Pardon! When Presbyterians have come to England for two or three years meaning to go back to Scotland, and remain Presbyterians, I have not felt able to admit them to our Communion, as they are not confirmed, nor do they wish to be.

I am afraid the same applies to Lutherans. If they are likely to stay in England, and wish to be confirmed, of course there would be no difficulty.

Could not your friend get to Grimsby now and again for her Communion in the Scandinavian Church? (Chapman Street, Grimsby). I am very sorry. How are you? My love to you both. . .

LXII.

ON THE MARRIAGE OF ONE UNBAPTISED.

LINCOLN, *May* 23, 1890.

I have thought over the difficult case which you send me of the unbaptised young man. I think it would be unreal to marry him in the Church with our service before he is baptised. Baptism is the covenanted basis of all the sacramental acts which are given in the Church.

I am sorry to disappoint him, but, if he cannot be baptised first, I should advise his marriage at the registry, which is valid marriage, and hope that he would some day after Baptism and Confirmation receive the Blessing of the Church.

With regard to the other sad case, I do not see what we can do unless they are willing to live apart, except withhold the Communion until it may be desired *in articulo mortis*.

These are sad cases, and one feels deeply for them, but we are guardians of the Faith and Sacraments.

LXIII.

TO A PRIEST—A CASE OF DISCIPLINE.

OLD PALACE, LINCOLN.

A.'s was a very bad case, and has caused a grievous scandal amongst us. He has been in debt in more than one place in the diocese, and in the county gaol till within a few months ago.

While I freely agree to his being accepted as a penitent to the Holy Communion, I feel that it would be a very serious shock to Church people if it were known that he was celebrating at the altar. A person whose moral sense has been so shattered requires the help of discipline to enable him to realise his sin; for his own sake, therefore, I could not allow him to celebrate the Holy Communion.

I fear you may think me hard; but, alas! experience teaches one the need of discipline in such cases.

I hope you are all keeping well.

God bless you, and guide you, and refresh you, with the increasing consciousness of His presence and His love.

P.S.—I fully appreciate B.'s Christian kindness towards A., but I am sure he would wish me to maintain the discipline of the Church, painful as it is to do it.

LXIV.

A DISPENSATION.

OLD PALACE, LINCOLN, *January* 29, 1906.

Thank you, and as this year will probably be a special occasion, and you may wish to please the officers, I will dispense you from keeping the Lenten fast on that occasion.

As a rule, I quite agree, we ought, by our examples as well as precepts, to uphold the rules of the Church.

May God guide and bless your work.

LXV.

TO A LADY—A RULE OF LIFE.

OXFORD, *December* 17, 1874.

I will gladly offer you the best advice I can.

1.—As to "Unregulated ways."

You can only expect in a life in the world to bring our minor features under rule, *e.g.*,

(1) Hours for sleep—going to bed and getting up.
(2) Meals (time, quantity, quality).
(3) Work.
(4) Devotion.
(*a*) Private.
(*b*) Public.

These main features of the day may be ascertained in most circumstances, so as to have an average of regularity.

2.—Working only for self-improvement.

(1) You cannot tell *when*, or *where*, your own powers may be called forth. Fénélon spent *ten* years of his life in teaching young religious women, but the result of his experience so gained was the so-called cause of his appointment to be tutor to the king's son. We cannot tell. If as far as you can tell from your own reason and conscience and the advice of others, you see nothing else to

do than improve yourself, do it heartily, not for self (as though God had let you off His service), but *for Him*; getting ready and making yourself as useful as you can for the time when He may call you to some more direct work for Himself.

3.—"Repeating Faults."

(1) It depends what they are.

(2) The Lord's Prayer seems to imply them, with a daily need and a daily debt.

(3) Sometimes a change of circumstances, place, occupation, companions, is helpful to get a closer line drawn between little failings and the right state.

(4) Confession.

I can only repeat the Church's advice, try and get on without it; if you can't, use it.

God guide and bless you.

LXVI.

MYSTICISM.

August 9, 1904.

I am so sorry I have been so long in thanking you for your most kind and loving letter, and for the exceedingly interesting and valuable book,[1] which you have been so good as to send me. How you must have valued and enjoyed the friendship of such a man.

There is a great deal that is most inspiring; indeed, the whole of his personality and tone of mind is so. And I hope to keep it by me to keep me up on the high spiritual level. There is just one caution, I venture to think, needed. It is a characteristic, much of that line of thought, the danger of running into a kind of ethical Pantheism, I mean the danger of losing the self to the degree of extinction by absorption. I have noticed the same in Westcott, and ——, and Moberly in different degrees.

It was the danger of Quietism, and even Fénélon was thought to have sympathised with it too much. No doubt most of us are only too far the other way, and are only beginning to see the perfection of the individual through corporate union.

I think if one takes the highest possible standard, we have the true safeguard: "*One as we* are one"—that is, with the ineffable distinctions of the Three Divine Personalities.

[1] Forbes Robinson's *Addresses*.

Pardon all these ill-natured remarks, but I only make them because I have so much comfort and encouragement in your sympathy that I point out a possible danger as a proof of my love. I am very sorry you have not been feeling quite well, but I hope Montana will quite set you up. That is where we first met!

Please remember me most kindly to your dear wife, and the dear children, and also to your friend whom I confirmed. I am so glad and thankful that he keeps on so well.

We shall be delighted to have you with us in the house for the Retreat. Good-bye. Keep out in the air all you can.

God bless you, and guide you, and lead you on, and give you grace to teach others.

Believe me always,
Yours most affectionately.

LXVII.

RESPECTING A YOUNG MAN IN AN OFFICE WHO FOUND HIMSELF COMPELLED TO MAKE MISLEADING STATEMENTS IN HIS CORRESPONDENCE, YET WISHED TO BE CONFIRMED.

October 31, 1905.

These cases are so difficult and sad; they belong to one of our greatest national difficulties and hindrances to the work of the Church. On the whole, my experience has worked like this: A baptised person ought to be confirmed, but the Church does not say exactly *when*. I fear to tell a young person to silence their conscience; it opens such a dangerous door. I should, therefore, advise the young man to *wait*, asking God's special help and protection, and hope that a way will be made clear for him in time. I should tell him, in case of sudden sickness and fear of death, to make known his case to a priest, and ask for Holy Communion. It is very hard. My love and blessing to you all.

LXVIII.

NONCONFORMISTS.

LONDON, *November* 4, 1906.

Let me thank you very warmly for your letter; and, though I do not feel able to do what you kindly wish, believe me I am heartily with you in your desire to promote good will and brotherly love amongst all men, and especially among Christian men. I need hardly say I have never had any harsh feeling towards Nonconformists, and, I might add, especially not towards Wesleyans and Primitive Methodists, because I have always felt that it was the want of spiritual life in the Church and brotherly love which led them to separate. The more we can draw near to Christ ourselves and fill ourselves with His Spirit, the greater power we shall have for unity. What we want is more *Christlike Christians*.

May God guide and bless your efforts to draw all nearer to Him, and in Him to one another.

LXIX.

TO A PRIEST—ON THE CELIBACY OF THE CLERGY.

LINCOLN, *June* 8, 1887.

As to the important matter on which you ask my advice, I will say that I think S. Paul puts before us the unmarried life as the higher state; but then, you must remember, he adds "for those who are called to it."

If you had been living as you were, or, if you thought the higher life would help your ministry best, then I should advise you to try for it. I gather, however, from your letter that you think a married priest would do most good in the sphere to which you have been called. I think, then, you are quite free to marry. I need not add "only in the Lord," which, as you know, would mean someone who would understand your priestly life and help you in it.

I am single myself, but simply because I never felt called to anything else.

I have the highest view of married life; indeed, I believe our English parsonages for purity of life may well compare with the old monasteries and the modern clergy houses.

I should make it a matter of prayer, and feel quite free. That God may guide you to know and do His Will is the sincere prayer of yours affectionately.

LXX.

SUFFERING.

LINCOLN, *Sunday.*

Thank you for telling me. I do indeed sympathise with you. But our likeness to our dear Lord is not complete unless we may suffer.

I like to think that the glorious visions of the Apocalypse were given in a time of suffering, at the end of a life. *We* may expect "good wine" at the last. How unlike the way of the world! I will not forget to think of you and your dear sister. May He Who knows best do His Will.

With my kindest regards and sympathy,

Yours affectionately.

LXXI.

TO ONE WHO HAD RECENTLY BEEN APPOINTED TUTOR IN A MISSIONARY COLLEGE.

CHRIST CHURCH, OXFORD, *September* 11, 1880.

You remember the songs of the "goings up" beginning "*When I was in trouble,*" so I am happy, and hopeful, that you have begun more or less in *misery*.

Dearest friend, I long at once to offer myself as junior Boots, or as something in the establishment, where I should be allowed instantly and always free access among the men. I quite envy you seeing such a lot of work that obviously wants doing close to your hand. It is delightful to know that you are in it.

But, seriously, I am sorry things are so needlessly stiff. There must be an immense loss of power. I should aim at absolute *oneness*, all higgledy piggledy. Anyhow, that must be the end to aim at. Meanwhile, it is true, no doubt, that a Christian higgledy piggledy is easier at Oxford or at Cuddesdon than at ——. The different social power must be a serious difficulty, and probably you will have to feel your way keeping up old-fashioned social barriers before you can safely trust to their perceiving the necessary order and harmony in a real Christian community. It will want *heaps* of *talk*—MOUNTAINS of talk—with individuals, and you will have to be worn out and out, and done for, and broken-hearted, and miserable, and not understood, and deceived, before you begin to get the right sort of relation which is absolutely necessary for the students' sake *now*, and to enable them to know what to do when they go out, be ordained, and preach, and give meditations; and get them to see that you are heart and soul in earnest to bring them one and all, not to yourself but to the mind of Christ. Then they will love you, and you will soon be hopelessly entangled in helpless love for them, and you will be broken-hearted again, and suffer miseries, and then the life will begin!

Dearest friend, you will think I am wild, but it would take three or four sheets to get off the first necessary wild confusion at thinking of such a place as ——, bound hand and foot in Donism. Horrible!

Yet be *patient*, and wise, and *work with others*. Do not be tempted to break away, but lead all on together, or as many as will. Pray write again, and I will be more sensible next time.

God bless and guide you, and fill you with wisdom and love to guide and love them all, and the heathen in them.

LXXII.

TO THE SAME.

OXFORD, *September* 10, 1881.

I am sorry you are so *squeezed*, but it must be so, more or less. Anyone who has a high ideal and love of perfection must be prepared to suffer. I am very fond of the Prophets. Among other things, they seem to have suffered a great deal. "Sat down astonied," or "dumb," or "sat in silence seven days," all implying the strain consequent upon a higher and wider vision. So no doubt S. James is right in telling us to take the Prophets as examples of PATIENCE. At first one fancies they had a brilliant time of it, but I expect not really. Do you know Ezekiel? He is the prophet of *hope* to me, the *rainbow* and *brightness round about*. The prophet Ezekiel, with his vision of the dry bones, and the water increasing, flowing from the Temple, is full of progress and hope. The Prophets are a great help to me. So you must not be in despair, dear friend. By degrees you will, please God, get on.

I should make a quiet gentle push to get Friday Meditations. One slides away from personal piety so very easily and in so many respectable ways, that unless there is a systematic consideration of the unseen spiritual life there is always danger of even a religious community becoming mere "Multus religionis nullius paene pietatis," as someone has said.

What you want is simple elementary instruction on

"How to be good," just enlivened and made bright and attractive by the personal experience of the man who gives it, and anecdotes from biographies, so as to make it *living, personal, touching*. I think you would all find the good of it. If the Warden did not like always to take it, you might divide it out amongst yourselves, only keep simple! . . .

Don't over worry, dear friend, and yet you must have a share in the sufferings, depression and amazements of the Prophets if you are really to lead men in the way of God.

God bless you, and comfort you, and guide you, and refresh you with the consciousness of His loving presence. . . .

LXXIII.

TO THE SAME.

OXFORD, *November* 23, 1882.

Dearest, dearest thing! I am so sorry for you, and yet it *must, must* be. Oh, you would not be worth your salt in such a place. Only by breaking your poor heart into pieces over and over again can you hope to make them begin to think of believing that there is such a thing as love!

Don't mind, be miserable, but don't stop loving them. And don't go to Africa just yet—come and see us first.

How I wish I could help you, but I can only say you will never regret *all* the misery you go through; and it is not lost, no, not one bit of it. Not one drop of heart's blood that falls from a love-broken heart ever gets lost; angels look after it if men don't, and it bears its fruit.

Trust, dear friend, and love on, and don't forget in your prayers sometimes.

Your very affectionate.

LXXIV.

TO ONE OF HIS CHAPLAINS—MISSIONARY WORK.

May, 1890.

I am off to China by the first boat! Will you come? I am just back from the meeting where a beautiful C.M.S. missionary straight from China has been preaching—at least what *I* call preaching—talking the Gospel with all the fervour of a living missionary. Most crushing! Eleven years and no results, and five deaths! Then three converts, and then another death! Then another year, and then 7,000! And such beauties! My dear child, if you and I get just in, it will be only by holding on to the extremest tip of one of their pigtails! Certainly those C.M.S. people have got a hold of "the faith in Jesus," which is most refreshing and vivifying. I could only think of that line in Keble for to-day,

"Not quite an outcast if I prove."[1]

We must really wake up. But this was meant to have been quite a sobér letter of thanks, dear thing, for all your help and *niceness* these last days. God bless you for it, and your work, and make them a blessing to thousands of millions. God bless you and support you.

[1] *The Christian Year.* First Sunday after Easter.

LXXV.

TO A LADY WHO, IN UNDERTAKING NEW WORK, WAS ACTING RATHER AGAINST WHAT THE BISHOP HAD ADVISED.

LINCOLN, *January* 9, 1900.

I thank you very much for your kind letter, though the responsibility weighs heavily upon me. Still, I offered the best contribution that I had, and I offered it *as a contribution* to help you to make up your own mind, and I am still of the same opinion. You are quite at liberty to tell A. that you have my full approval in remaining. I feel that you have a very real and valuable work to do here, and that it would be vastly easier to find some one to take up the work for the Grey Ladies than the work here, which depends so much on your own personality and family connections. I ought, perhaps, to say that I may be too much inclined to follow the natural setting of life. I see so much danger in humanly devised religious organisations. Simplicity, quietness, real looking to God and living with Him are all so easily endangered, even by religious organisations. I only say this that you may guard yourself against what may be prejudices.

May God guide and bless your decision, to your own happiness and the highest good of others,

LXXVI.

WHEN ASKED TO BE PATRON OF A CHORAL SOCIETY WHICH PROPOSED TO GIVE PERFORMANCES OF ORATORIOS ON SUNDAY.

January 30, 1905.

It is long indeed since I heard of you, but I remember you quite well, and your good father.

I am very sorry not to feel able to do what you ask. For your sake I should be very glad to do it, but I hesitate to promote a movement which, however good in itself, may be abused by leading people to substitute listening even to sacred music for going to church.

I know there are two sides to the question, but I have an old-fashioned jealousy for the religious Sunday, and am afraid of doing anything that might lessen its religious power. I am sure you yourself desire to do good, and to keep people from harm. May God guide and bless you in your effort.

LXXVII.

TO ONE OF HIS YOUNGER CLERGY—ON HIS DESIRE TO JOIN THE SOCIETY OF S. JOHN THE EVANGELIST, COWLEY.

April 14, 1891.

Ah! You naughty child! I was afraid you would flit off and leave me with my poor lads and the turnips!

Well, dear child, I will not hinder you. If we are to have Religious, you are just the sort of child to make the life, by God's grace, what it ought to be. So you must go, if you think you ought, and God bless you, though I am very sorry to lose you.

God bless you, my dear child, and guide you,

LXXVIII.

TO A YOUNG PRIEST—ON HOME LIFE.

September, 1888.

I am very glad you have been at home and seen and felt as you have; whenever home breaks up (as, alas! it must) you will look back to this summer as a gift of pause before the end, and as a real and wonderful ordering of the "Father of all." What our behaviour to Him must be in His sight is beyond all imagination!

I quite understand and agree about the feelings of wonder and awe and admiration at a Mother's courage and self-effacing love, and the pain inexpressible when children show "unconcern." The sight of all this cannot but give you a new and most real reverence and self-hating tenderness towards the mystery of family life; and this, dear child, is just what I want you to get, not that you should necessarily be *married*, any more than I am, but that you should increase in self-hating reverence for others, and grow in the general apprehension that others are a few million times better than oneself and only to be interfered with with awe!

But I might spare you all this, as we shall (D.V). so soon meet. I am thankful for my holiday, which has been a real refreshment, and I hope to try to do a little better. I see some things, I hope, a little clearer, if I can only keep down the dust of daily toil and manage to retain my own individuality without selfishness. Any kind of public life must be a self-sacrifice. "He saved others, *Himself* He cannot save," is true of all who would try to follow Him. *Smashing* is in the bond, though it may not be exacted to the full.

Good-bye; God bless you and guide you.

LXXIX.

TO A PRIEST OF THE DIOCESE—ON COMMUNION WITH GOD.

LINCOLN, *May* 15, 1885.

Thank you for your trustful letter.

I shall be only too glad and thankful if I can help you as you propose. Indeed, it is my great wish, if it please God, to help on clergy of the diocese into peaceful communion with God, that they may then be enabled to do the same for their people. When you come we will find a time for you to tell me all you wish. It is not all at once, very often, that we can attain that even and consistent living with God which in His time may be ours; and which, when attained, is such a rest.

That this may be yours, and that you may be enabled to bring others to the same is my sincere prayer.

God bless you and comfort you.

LXXX.

TO A WORKING MAN.

OLD PALACE, LINCOLN, *September* 3, 1909.

As I am staying at Folkestone for a few days I have a little more leisure time than when I am at Lincoln, so I am writing to thank you for your kind letter of last January. I hope you keep well, and all your family, and that they are all well in the old home at ———. Remember me very highly to your father when you see him, or are writing, and give my love to Edward and Willie; I hope they are well, and doing well both in soul and body. It wants a deal of energy and courage to keep up to the mark in religion nowadays. There are so many good-living people who are almost indifferent to religion. It is very dangerous, and sometimes very sad when they suddenly break down altogether. The world goes ahead wonderfully—railways, telegraph, telephone, steamships, and now aviation; we must hold fast by the faith, or there will be a great smash. I am not against worldly progress, but it must be *with God* and *for God*, or it will have to be stopped.

God bless you, dear [Tom], and all your family.

THE LETTER OF THE FOREGOING

To the Rev. B. W. Randolph.

Dear Sir,

Seeing your letter in the daily Press *re* the late Bishop of Lincoln's Spiritual Letters from him, I had the great honour of knowing him the whole of my life through me being a native of Leigh, where his dear brother, the late Canon King, was Rector. My father was one of his Sunday School teachers there until the time of his death, and one of my brothers, Willie, was a servant of his, and went with him as his servant to Christ Church from Cuddesdon. You may, perhaps, remember him, as he was at Oxford some years with him. And then a younger brother, Edward, went to Cuddesdon as a servant afterwards. You will see by this how it is I knew him so well, for when he used to visit his brother at Leigh he always used to call on us at our home.

We met in London some thirty years since, when we promised to write each other, say, once a year, just to keep in touch with each other. Our letters were very homely ones, really about our family, and would not interest other people, but the last one that I send you may be of interest to you.

I may say that I am a working man; have been in my present place close on thirty years; also a Sunday School teacher, though, perhaps, this is not to my credit, rather to my dear ones and teachers who have passed to their rest. That I may live a life here below so that at the last I am found worthy to meet them all, is the very earnest prayer of

Yours sincerely,
TOM ——

LXXXI.

TO SOME FRIENDS WITH WHOM HE HAD TRAVELLED—THANKING FOR PRESENTS.

LINCOLN, *January* 14, 1891.

If *you* were not YOU I should really seriously fear that you would be offended at my apparent ingratitude! But I know how kind you are, and you also know that the reason of my silence is really pressure of work on one who never was very strong, and who is getting old and not, I fear, more active.

But how am I to thank you even if I try? It is really too good of you to shower such beautiful and valuable presents upon me.

The *bag* is most beautiful, and I am sure will impress the various footmen in the houses where I stay with a much higher idea of their Bishop than they get now from my poor black bag which you so often helped me with.

And then the wonderful wrapper for my rugs, and umbrellas, and stick cases! People will not know me! I have often wished for (not to say coveted) such a luxury when I have been struggling with my bulging bundles of rugs and coats!

I quite long to set off again. It makes me blush to think how you struggled with my bundles last autumn.

And what am I to say for the charmingly arranged book of photographs? So full of memories! It is too good of you. The cow and the bell, I think, must come first, and you are both excellent, and the hay cart is a great memory, and your own home, which is a pleasure yet to come for me. I think the photographs excellent. It is really wonderful. And then after all this came the book on *Socialism*, as if you had nothing to do but think about my interest and pleasure! And then all your letters and good wishes.

Well, dear friends, it is impossible to thank you, and under all lies the great joy of all that all this is bound up with Church principles, and is part of the enjoyment of the Communion of Saints. I hope you have had a happy Christmas. I fear your anxiety for your good sister-in-law must have made your Christmas grave, but not, I hope, unhappy. Such Christian resignation and hope are the elements of encouragement and joy.

I am with my sister at C. for five days, but go home to-morrow.

I am waiting to see what the appeal will come to. I do not mean to defend the judgment before the P.C., but to stand on the decision of the Archbishop of Canterbury. This will, I think, be the clearest course for Church people to understand.

If I am not in gaol you must come to me for Easter! Good-bye, dear friends, my love and blessing to you both.

May God bless you for your kindness to His servant. . . .

LXXXII.

BIBLE READING.

CHRIST CHURCH, OXFORD, *December* 31, 1883.

What little I know about it I should say a *mixed* [method is best].

The critical often keeps one awake, opens one's eyes. Only remember, dear Charles Marriott says:—

"The utmost that criticism can do is to prepare and correct text for the reading of the spiritual age."

Still, I think it often opens one's eyes. I mean, without a commentary one does not crack the nut. I want you to teach me a great deal when you come to ——.

Let us try and begin to get hold of *something*. I think I have begun to see my way to the alphabet of morality, but I have hardly begun Christianity, and I was *fifty-four* on Saturday! God bless you and guide you through the new year, and on and on!

Yours affectionately.

LXXXIII.

TO A LADY—ON FASTING COMMUNION.

LINCOLN, *Febuary*, 19, 1905,
Septuagesima.

I am sorry you are distressed about the matter of which you write. I do not think you need be so any more. No doubt the first aim of us all should be to receive the Holy Communion as our first food in the day—that is, fasting.

But that rule should be subject to the higher law of *equity*, and in cases of sickness or constitutional weakness or old age a person should be dispensed from it, either by a formal dispensation, or, if that cannot be readily obtained, by trusting to God's loving mercy, Who never requires us to do more than we can. I am sure you will do well to take what will enable you to receive the Blessed Sacrament without injury to your health, or causing you undue anxiety about your body.

I should advise you to do this and not to diminish the number of your Communions.

May God guide and bless you.

LXXXIV.

TO THE MEMBERS OF THE GUILD OF S. BARNABAS FOR NURSES.

THE OLD PALACE, LINCOLN,
Christmas, 1888.

I think it a very great privilege to be in any way connected with you, because you are the special friends of the suffering. In the great day of Judgment, the Saviour says that those who have waited upon the sick in a right spirit will be surprised to find that they are saved. You have many trials, many temptations, many spiritual privations, but Jesus is watching you, and if you will look to Him, and keep with Him as He has told you in His Holy Church, you need not be afraid, but work on bravely in the midst of sadness and suffering of body and mind, looking forward to the rest and glory which are not far off.

May God give you strength of body and spirit for your blessed work through the New Year, and may your skilful, tender, patient love lead those to whom you minister to the knowledge of the love of God.

Accept my blessing on yourselves, and for those to whom you minister. God bless you and keep you.

LXXXV.

TO THE SAME.

THE OLD PALACE, LINCOLN, *January*, 1898.

When I look back over the year which is so nearly gone, I can see nothing but the unexpected and rare delight of our Festival at S. Barnabas, at the end of June—that still remains in my memory as an epoch in my life. It seems to shut out all other things connected with our Guild. It seemed to me like a dream realised in the Church of England—a dream of beauty, and holiness, and self-sacrificing love, such as we dreamed of some forty years ago, but hardly hoped to see, and now the dream has come true, and far more. "So He giveth His beloved (in) sleep."

Those of you who were there, will remember the service in the church, the Te Deum, and all that the good Vicar did for us; and all that your dear chaplain said and did, with all his natural grace and sanctified love. It was a realised dream to me, for which I cannot express my thanks.

I have been told that it might perhaps be helpful to some of you if I were to give you some thoughts this year on the value of *Conversation*.

I have often handed on to you some wise sayings from Bishop Butler, who has been one of my life-long and most valued companions. He has a wonderful sermon on "The government of the tongue."

It is not to the *negative* warnings which he gives, that I think it needful to call your attention, the dangers of not "bridling the tongue." These arise mainly from three causes, as you know:

(1) Not observing the obvious occasions of silence.
(2) Not checking the propensity to tale-bearing, and unduly talking over people's characters.
(3) Not subduing the eager desire to gain attention, which appears to be an original disease in some.

But it is upon the *positive* side of conversation, its *value* rather than its danger, that I wish to speak.

"The chief purpose (Bishop Butler observes) for which the faculty of speech was given man, is plainly that we might communicate our thoughts to each other, for business, and for our improvement in knowledge and learning. But the good Author of our nature has not only provided us with things which are necessary, but also with many things for our enjoyment and comfort.

"Besides the necessary light which He has given us for our work, He has given us an endless variety of pleasures, through the beauty of colour and form, in the clouds, and in the flowers, and in people's faces.

"There are *secondary* uses of our faculties. They administer to *delight* as well as to *necessity*. The secondary use of speech is to please, and to be entertaining to each other."

I can easily imagine that in your work, "conversation" may form one of your dangers, or opportunities for great good.

The first great governing rule we may take from the

Book of books, Proverbs xxxi. 26, "She openeth her mouth with wisdom, and in her tongue is the law of kindness." These are the essential conditions of edifying conversation; to be "sensible and kind." But under the word *wisdom*, much may be included; it is here spoken of as the mark of a woman's lips, yet the same word is used to express the knowledge of Solomon; a very wide field indeed is open to you.

The difficulty is how practically to make use of the opportunity.

Perhaps the first thing is for you to try and realise that by fitting yourselves for the opportunities of conversation, you would be adding another qualification for your work.

The method of fitting yourselves would be, I suppose, by increasing your general knowledge through reading. You must not be disappointed if you cannot do very much; still, it is wonderful how much may be done when there is the will.

Your *line* of reading should be determined by your own natural inclination. There are different lines for you to choose between: poetry, biographies, histories, together with stories chosen, whichever interests you most; your time for reading will be necessarily very broken and irregular, but where there is a will there is a way. Our true love does not mind waiting, and being interrupted; it is always *there*, and *ready* when the opportunity comes.

However, whatever you may do in this way, remember that its real value will depend upon the rectitude of your real self, your inner motive. That motive many a poor patient will be able to perceive and appreciate, though they very soon fall asleep under your attempts to raise the standard of conversation. They will know when you are really unselfish in your efforts, they will appreciate the absence of frivolity, and any want of charity, if you always open "your mouth with wisdom," and if "the law of kindness" rules your tongue.

They will notice if you *never* touch upon things that are unholy, and are always ready if invited to talk on holy things.

Such an inner rectitude is, you know well, only to be maintained by the aid of the Holy Spirit, by frequent prayer, by the study of God's Word, by strengthening and refreshing your soul through the Blessed Sacrament at the Altar, and by careful attendance to your own rules.

I do not know whether what I have written will be any help to you; but at least you will see that I am anxious to do anything that might, in however small a degree, make your good work better.

It is with the greatest thankfulness and hope, that I still hear the same high report of your lives, and of your work.

Your loving, self-devoted lives are a constant witness to me (for which I have no words to express my thankfulness) of the presence of Christ in His Church.

May God continue to guide and bless you, and those to whom you minister.

LXXXVI.

TO THE SAME.

OLD PALACE, LINCOLN, *December* 20, 1909.

Yet once more, by God's mercy, I am allowed to write to you!

First let me express my thanks to Almighty God for this continued goodness towards us. I hear our numbers have entered the fifth thousand! That is very wonderful, as you are not drawn together like the members of a money-making insurance company, but simply by the power of the faith, and the golden cord of God's love.

And then, next, let me thank you for perseverance in your work, though in the constant presence of sickness, and suffering, and death.

I have nothing new to say to you, my dear children in Christ, but I have just been reading a book addressed to clergymen, which puts one side of the truth with fresh vigour. He says his book "starts from the truth that there is an Incarnation in the priest which is to save the parish." "That Christ is in the priest reconciling the parish unto God."

This is said specially of the clergy, but it is also true of you, and of every true Christian man and woman. It is your great work to bring the Likeness, and Mind, and Spirit of Christ into the sick room, into every ward in the hospital, and into every mind and heart of every sick person in the ward.

It is your great privilege to represent the sympathy

and the love of Christ, and to show how they can live independently of earthly reward, without the praise of men or the surroundings of luxury. You attend with patient cheerfulness the sick and the poor, the thankful and the unthankful, the patient and the complaining. In the Spirit of Christ you can "Weep with those who weep," and "Rejoice with those who rejoice." In the children's ward you can play with the children, and help to make them happy. You bring amongst them the spirit of Him Who made the marriage feast of Cana cheerful through His first miracle. Into the chamber of suffering and death you bring the spirit of Him Who wept by the grave of Lazarus. Your unfailing care and tenderness for the sick and dying will be an evidence to them that you value life for something beyond its use in this world. Your calmness and steady confidence in the hour of death will help them to lay firm hold of the "Sure and certain hope of the resurrection to eternal life."

Let this be your New Year's thought, "I am to carry on the great work of the Incarnation."

This is no mere fancy, but the truth based upon the great words of Scripture, "The Word was made Flesh, and dwelt among us, and we beheld His Glory, the glory as of the only-begotten of the Father, full of grace and truth. . . . And of His fulness have we all received." Through the Incarnation God and man are linked together most mysteriously, so that our Saviour could say, "Inasmuch as ye did unto one of the least of these My brethren, ye did it unto Me."

Your prayers, your Bible, and the Blessed Sacrament are the great means by which this precious truth is kept alive in your minds and hearts. It is a supernatural truth—a truth of God's special revelation: see that you are careful to make full use of the supernatural means by which the great truth is retained.

May God continue and abide with you, and bless you, and refresh you with the increasing consciousness of His presence and His love.

LXXXVII.

ON FRIENDSHIP.

LINCOLN, *January* 2, 1888.

Thank you so much for your kind note, and good wishes for the new year. I most heartily return them. Few things are a greater comfort and support, as one gets on in life, than sincerity in friendship. There seems to be many outward forms of friendship—*ecclesiastical*—an attempt to love everyone; *political*—a form of mere ambition; but the real disinterested, pure, genuine Christian friend is a real comfort and support, and such you have been, dear friend, all these twenty-eight years! It sounds a long time; and yet I can go back in memory to those Cuddesdon days without any effort. They seem to live on with me.

I am so glad you are well. There is nothing like Switzerland. I was in the Engadine last year (1887), and enjoyed it immensely. Do you know it? The air is splendid.

God bless you, dear friend, and guide and comfort you and your flock through the New Year and many more.

I am, yours ever affectionately.

LXXXVIII.

THE BURDEN OF LIFE.

May 26, 1904.

Your letter was a great pleasure and comfort to me. I have been somewhat hard pressed lately with work and worries, and your loving words reminded me of old days, and revived the old spirit of hope.

I wish I could help you, dearest man, with a Curate. I will keep you in mind, and let you know with pleasure if I find anyone.

I am so sorry for your disappointment and worry with ——. Life is a great discipline. Indeed, at times it seems almost more than one can bear. For me it gets easier in one way that it cannot be much longer. If I can only hold on till it pleases God to say "It is enough!"

Ah! dearest old child, when one looks back at one's old ideals, I am afraid one sees one may have thought too much of oneself, and been too ambitious. A humbler, quieter life might have been safer, but one did not know what was coming, and so went on step by step, and now one sees how much there is to be done that one cannot do!

Pardon such selfish thoughts, but the constancy of your love will always be one of my most real comforts.

How simple our old Cuddesdon life was! But how real and happy!

Shall you be at Cuddesdon?

How are you?

With my love and blessing.
Believe me always, your most affectionate.

LXXXIX.

PAGEANTS.

June 28, 1909.

I am conscious of having felt something uncomfortable at the thought of the clergy *acting*. I certainly cannot imagine dear Lord Alwyne, or Dean Church, dressing up, and posing to be looked at by hundreds of people! and they, and such as they, have been our elevating models. But I feel also that this way of acting, and putting pictures into all the newspapers, is a concession to the weakness of the general mental power of the public. They have not power, apparently, to realise truth except through the eye. It seems to suggest want of mental power and imagination, not to say "laziness" and "hurry." So I have never been to any pageant, and I hope they will not want one here in my time. But, having said all this, I am quite willing that they should go on (I am not quite sure about the clergy acting), and I hope they will encourage people to read and try to exercise their minds more. Examinations, and lectures, and reviews tend very much to lead people to live upon *other people's thoughts*. You remember Cowper:—

"Knowledge and wisdom, far from being one,
Have ofttimes no connection. Knowledge dwells
In heads replete with thoughts of other men,
Wisdom is minds attentive to their own."
(THE TASK—*The Winter Walk at Morn*).

I wish people would read Cowper, and Wordsworth, and Crabbe.

But I forget that I am writing and not talking.

XC.

TO A FRIEND—WORDSWORTH'S POEMS.

LINCOLN, *December* 23, 1897.

There are only two people I can think of on this side of Paradise who would think of giving a Christmas present *in eight volumes!* So I write at once to thank you with all my heart for the wonderful continuance of your love and goodness to me, and all about me. It is a most beautiful and usable Wordsworth, and I am particularly glad to have it, as he seems to suit me. His love of all nature, and his constant use of it are a link to higher things which I greatly love; and his philosophical reflections, which some might think heavy, and others not purely metaphysical enough, just suit my capacities, so his poetry rests and refreshes me with new strength of head and heart, of thought and love. I shall often take a volume about with me.

How are you all? I trust well, and happy, and making all round you happy, I have no doubt. We are all well, D.G.

With my love, and best Christmas blessings.

XCI.

TO A LAY READER OF THE DIOCESE WHO HAD SENT HIM A COPY OF AN ADDRESS TO SUNDAY SCHOOL TEACHERS.

September 10, 1906.

Thank you very much for sending me your address for the Sunday School teachers. You are quite right, "Love" is the golden thread which God wants us to use. It will draw us to Himself and to one another. God bless you and your work.

XCII.

TO A PRIEST—ON THE DEATH OF HIS SISTER.

OXFORD, *January* 8, 1875.

I must send a hurried line to assure you of my sincere and affectionate sympathy. I remember your sister so well! I am sure you feel dreadfully cut in two, in spite of all the true comfort! for one does feel a dreadful void, and sinking sickness, in sorrow which rends the heart. Just now I seem to realise it, because we are in great anxiety about my dear brother's eldest boy, who we fear has been lost off the West Coast of Africa. My poor brother will be dreadfully distressed; yet, dearest friend, this is the divine reality of the discipline we are under. We may be sure it is right, right for them who go before, and right for us who are left. It helps us to keep detached, and makes life more a *Passage*, and helps us to give up the idea of resting here, and so we meet troubles better.

God bless you, dearest friend, and comfort you and give you strength to bear this trial, that it may bear its full fruit. . . .

XCIII.

TO A PRIEST—ON CONFESSION.

CHRIST CHURCH, *February* 14, 1883.

Thank you for your letter, which I have read and destroyed.

First, as to the general question of going to confession, or not.

As you have been, and no doubt would wish for it if you were ill, I should say you were free to go, or not to go, in between, assuming that you would go in this intermediate time, if you felt any particular need.

I should say you were free to go or not, under these circumstances, as you judge it will be best for you.

But, as you ask what I should advise, I can only add:

People are very differently constituted. To some going to confession is a great effort, and strain, and seems to make a considerable demand on their nervous power. If this is so with you, and you are conscious of being over-scrupulous, it might be well to try your freedom for a year or two to see if you got stronger.

Another question would be whether you could go less frequently than you have done of late.

For myself, I go three or four times a year, not more, and I should have recommended you, therefore, something of the same kind.

In fact, subject to your own judgment, that would be my advice, to put aside all scruples as far as you can, make it as little a strain as you can. Do not feel bound to go, and yet, three times a year, or Advent and Lent, try to go.

Then, as to the person.

I can quite understand what you feel. I used to go to the dear Dr.,[1] but for some years, to save him trouble, I have always gone to Father ——. For this reason I should be inclined to recommend him to you. He is most simple, kind, and full of common sense, and not the least likely to encourage scruples, or to weaken anyone. The difficulty, perhaps, is catching him; but he is often in London, and he is always ready, poor dear man, if he is not actually engaged.

Of the other two I should think —— perhaps the best for a priest, as being both younger and more of a theologian. Be simple, dear friend, and trustful. God takes care of us, and sends us trouble to humble us. . . .

If I can help any further or at any time always write.

God bless you, and guide you, and help you to trust His love.

[1] Pusey.

XCIV.

TO ONE WHO HAD LOST HIS MOTHER.

LINCOLN, *June* 10, 1887.

I am so sorry for my delay in writing to you, not only about coming to you, as you kindly ask, but to assure you of my sincere sympathy with you in your great, great sorrow.

I wish I could come to you, but I am engaged to the full now, and I dare not add more. I was so grieved for you, and dear Reggie, when I heard of your terrible trouble. I know by experience how blank it makes things—no one to tell all the little things of interest to! No one to keep waiting for one and to help on one's self-planned plans! It is a terrible loss and blank. The point of unity in the family seems gone. But, dear friend, you *will* have help to bear it, and in time you will understand and see how all has been ordered in wisdom and in love.

Life never can be quite the same. But you would not wish to have it otherwise as you see the wisdom and the love which has ruled all.

A new nearness to God, a purer intention, a more direct living for the world beyond, a new freedom and sense of independence to the world, its frowns and smiles, and firmer courage; these, dear friend, are some of the gifts and consolation I believe you will find in God's good time. Meanwhile you can trust yourself to the prayers of the Church for those in "Trouble and sorrow."

My love and blessing to you and dear R.

Yours affectionately. . . .

XCV.

TO A FRIEND—ON THE DEATH OF HIS MARRIED DAUGHTER.

LINCOLN, *January* 17, 1889.

Thank you for your great kindness in allowing me so quickly to be with you in your great sorrow, for so it must be even to the most Christian heart. I had hoped, and prayed, that, if it pleased God, you might all be spared this great pain, but He Who did not withdraw the cup in the garden knows what is best. On *this* we may most surely rest, and in time, or in eternity, we shall *know* this. At present we may not be able to do more than accept and believe it, but such acceptance is surely most blessed in its fruits, for it is the union of our will with His Will, and this is a central point of the restoration of the divine likeness in us, and our especial preparation for our eternal communion in heaven. Through suffering we are perfected.

I am thankful to hear that you have all been sustained. I do not doubt that you will be, only I feel that the strain on the dear husband, and on dear Mrs.

V., and on you all must be terrible. But I do not doubt He will sustain you.

I return (D.V.) to-morrow. You will have made your arrangements for Saturday, but anything I could do you know I shall be glad to do. I shall be engaged in the morning, but free in the afternoon. I only say this, not to intrude, but to assure you of my readiness to express my sincere sympathy in any way I can.

God bless you and support you all.

I am, yours very affectionately.

XCVI.

TO A LADY—ON THE DEATH OF A SAILOR LAD.

LINCOLN, *December* 3, 1889.

Pardon my delay in returning these most interesting and precious letters. I have ventured to write a few unworthy words to poor Mrs. H., if you think it well to send them. I am sure you must have suffered very much from this sad occurrence. But I am sure you may have the greatest comfort. This world is so full of difficulty and danger that one could not wish any back again who have been taken while on the right path. They have been saved we know not from what dangers of the young which might have ruined them.

It is very difficult not to be quite brokenhearted when such sorrows come, and life seems almost impossible at times; but *He* Who is the Life can support us, and He will. It must be, I am sure, a very great pleasure and satisfaction to you to feel that you did so much for the dear lad, and that he has won such a good testimony. I have, you may like to know, on more than one occasion spoken of the good lad's life and death in my Confirmation addresses; so that the seed is scattered for a wider and continuing life, and not really lost. Please God, in Paradise we may meet those whose prayers and early death may have helped to bring us there.

May you, by God's blessing, one day join them, and then you will know that all your pain, and love, and sorrow were not in vain.

XCVII.

TO A FRIEND—DR. LIDDON'S FUNERAL.

LINCOLN, *September* 19, 1890.

I must thank you—this I cannot really do—for all your most indulgent care of me. I am afraid I was very selfish and distracting in return, but it was a great pleasure and comfort to me, and especially at the last. It will always mark our little tour together! St. Paul's was most wonderful. I never shall forget the effect of seeing the coffin carried from the choir down to the dome. It seemed to be floating on into a sea of living faces, which, in thousands, were gazing at it from every part of the great nave and dome. It looked like a foretaste of the welcome in Paradise. It was most beautiful. Good-bye! Please give my grateful thanks to your dear husband for all his loving care.

My love and blessing to you both. . . .

XCVIII.

ON THE DEATH OF DEAN CHURCH.

LONDON, *December* 9, 1890.

The good and great Dean of St. Paul's has gone, at least we cannot consult him as we used. It is very terrible. This last part of the pathway of one's life wants more courage and self-reliance than the earlier stages, where one had so many on either hand to consult. It teaches one terribly the folly of not living in the closest communion with God, the nothingness of popularity and human praise. Faith in Him and in His presence seem the only remedy against abject cowardice and flight. I have seen this more or less clearly all along, but the clouds of earthly things have left me more liable to fear than might have been.

What a beautiful life his was! so splendidly free from all this earthly dross and clouding; so pure, and, therefore, so strong. He seemed to combine the old Tractarian spirit of retirement with the highest and best modern culture and refinement. His wisdom and unostentatious knowledge were so wonderful.

His loss after dear Liddon's seems terrible. Perhaps it means that our natural strength is being reduced because God has some great victory to win for His Church, and may we not hinder it!

XCIX.

TO A LADY—ON THE DEATH OF HIS OWN SISTER.

OLD PALACE, LINCOLN, *July* 29, 1892.

I must add a word of special thanks to you for your kind words of sympathy.

You have had so much sorrow that you know what it is.

I feel as if I had been in a storm, and my sails were split, but sail mending is apostolic work, and I trust that God will give me skill and power to make them strong enough (when, after a bit, I put out to sea again) to finish my course.

Sorrow has its strengthening side, has it not? It seems to take away the dross of the fear and love of the world. I hope it may be so, and that I may, if it please God, have strength to serve the diocese better than I have done.

With my love and blessing.

C.

TO ONE WHOSE BROTHER HAD BEEN DROWNED AT SEA.

LINCOLN, *November* 2, 1892.

Your terrible letter reached me last evening. I don't know what to say; it is beyond all words. Just not to be quite stunned or fall is as much as you can hope for for the present, then it will become a new power to you. Your life won't be quite the same. What people call a *blow* leaves a mark, but for good under God.

I will write to your dear mother. What it must be to them we cannot think! But He, Who gave His only Son, *knows!*

God bless you, my dearest child, and support you through this suffering, and rest, and enable others to rest more completely in His love.

Always yours most lovingly. . . .

CI.

TO HIS COUSIN—ON THE DEATH OF HER SISTER.

April 29, 1894.

I have heard from Clevedon of your great loss and sorrow, and must write one word to assure you of my sincere sympathy. Dear A.'s life was one of great patience, but we must rejoice for her that now she has the full vision of Paradise without any veil between. May I say, dear cousin, how often I have expressed my admiration to my sisters at the way in which you have devoted your own life to take care of your dear sister? We all of our generation owe you a debt of gratitude for the example of unselfish devotion which you have set us. May He, Who only can, now be your stay and comfort! I am sure, after a little time, you will look back with thankfulness and comfort to the many years you have lived together, though it will be hard for you at first to know exactly what to do. There is a verse in the Psalms which has helped me sometimes: "I see that all things come to an end, but Thy Commandment is exceeding broad." In time you will see what His Will for you is, and then, I doubt not, find happiness in doing it again here on earth for a little longer, and then enjoy doing it for ever in heaven with those who have gone before.

May God bless and comfort you.

CII.

TO ONE WHO HAD LOST HIS FATHER.

September 18, 1899.

Thank you for your note.

I did not know that your dear father had been called away. It is a very unique epoch in one's life when that call comes, and life never seems quite the same after it. One loses the feeling of the safety of childhood, and seems thrust out into the cold. Yet it must be so, and we know it is God's own plan, and, therefore, the best. And, as you say, there are grounds for thankfulness that you have all been spared a long and painful watching. No doubt all is done well. R.I.P. I am sorry you cannot come for the Retreat. Would you like to come and stay with us for the Conference?

Please offer my sincere sympathy to your dear mother and sisters. God bless you and comfort you.

CIII.

TO A YOUNG MAN—ON THE DEATH OF HIS FATHER.

August 24, 1901.

I have seen in the papers what trouble you are in through the loss of your dear father, so I am venturing to write to assure you of my sincere sympathy.

I know by experience what a great event in one's life such a loss is—it seems to take away an old protection that one could feel safe under, and to push one out into the front, in the open as it were. I am sure you will feel it very much, dear man, not only for your own sake, but for the sake of your dear mother, for I think you told me she was living. The broken life of widowhood must be terrible; and yet the same Hand that made the two one can support them for a while apart, and then unite them together again for ever. May God uphold you all, dear friend, according to your different needs. He can, I know by experience, and I trust that He will. Then you will find that the withdrawal of this support will give you new strength, and though life will never look quite the same, yet you will feel that all is well done, and you will know the special sense of comfort and power that comes from Him as the God of the fatherless and widow. It will all help you to trust Him more and more. I am glad to think that you have the special love of *one* to comfort you. May God bless you both, and comfort you with the increasing consciousness of His presence and His love.

CIV.

TO A PRIEST—ON THE DEATH OF HIS CHILD.

OLD PALACE, LINCOLN, *April* 7, 1904.

I am very glad of the opportunity of expressing to you my very sincere sympathy in your recent most sad loss. I must express my regret that I did not write at once, but you know how fully my time is occupied.

One great consolation we may have in the death of the young, that they are taken away from the evil and trials of this life to the brighter and far happier life above. For them we may indeed feel thankful, but that it makes another shadow on the path of those who are still following on here below. Yet shadows are made by sunlight above, and I trust that God in His loving care will give the comfort and strength to you and Mrs. —— to follow bravely on till you meet again those who have gone before.

I am sorry to see that Mrs. —— has been ill, and hope, please God, she may soon regain her strength.

Believe me, with sincere sympathy.

CV.

TO A YOUNG LADY—ON THE DEATH OF HER BROTHER.

LINCOLN, *May* 11, 1904.

I am so sorry! I mean for all of us who are left; for dear Walter we know we may be glad and thankful. I like the phrase "The gate of death," and to think of it as the "garden gate" that opens into the "Garden of Paradise." There is rest and peace, and light, and sure and certain hope, of even greater glory.

Dear W. seemed so well when we met at Morton. I am so glad we met; he seemed so happy, and I was so glad to hear of his Bible Class. I am sure his life, and teaching, and now his early death, will touch many. It is a great thing to leave such a memory. But you, dear K., and your dear father and mother must miss him, I know, terribly. Please give my love to them, and assure them of my sympathy and my prayers, and Mr. W. joins with me in saying this, but both feel we have lost a friend. I am so glad you were with him, and able to read to him.

I shall think of the 23rd Psalm as his, and remember him. We cannot be too thankful that all was so peaceful, and that he was spared a long weary illness. God is indeed merciful. So, dear K., we must try and follow trustfully and bravely on, looking forward to meeting again.

God bless you and comfort you all.

CVI.

TO A LADY—ON THE DEATH OF HER BROTHER.

August 12, 1905.

Your kind letter telling me that your poor dear brother had passed away from us into the better world above has just reached me. I thank you very much for telling me. I was very anxious about him, and hoped he might have lived; but in truth he does live, and in a fuller and better life than we can live here. God often gives more than we ask or think. We asked life for him, and now God (we may truly believe) has given him a long life, even for ever and ever.

But, of course, I know you must all feel sad at losing him, and his poor widow especially. Will you say a kind word to her from me, and give her my blessing, and may God comfort her and take care of her? He is the God of the fatherless and widow. And may God comfort you yourself, and his mother and brothers. Death is not the end of life, but rather the beginning of the higher and better part of life. The collect for Easter Eve speaks of death as a "gate"—"through the grave and gate of death," and I like to think of death as a *garden gate* leading into Paradise, which is the garden of God. There all is bright and happy, and we may trust it is so with your dear brother. He set us all a good example, and we must try and follow on and look forward to meeting again.

CVII.

TO THE SAME—ON THE DEATH OF HER FATHER.

LINCOLN, *May* 17, 1909.

How good of you to write!

I am so sorry for you, and your dear mother; for your dear father we may indeed give thanks. It is far, far better to depart and to be with Him! Thank you for telling me of the beautiful example of his patience. We must try to follow on. It will be a great comfort to you that you have been able to help and comfort him so much at home, and your dear good husband too. My love to him. Give my love to your dear mother, and assure her of my prayers.

I shall always remember my happy visits to Hanthorpe; all will seem bewildering for a while. But in God's good time He will show you what He yet has for you to do. For the present, just trust to His mercy and rest in His love like a child. That is all we can do, and we *may* do it, and it is *enough!*

My love and blessing to you all. . . .

CVIII.

TO A FRIEND—ON THE DEATH OF HIS MOTHER.

December 18, 1905.

Thank you for telling me of your dear mother's call to the better world, R.I.P. But you will feel the loss, I know. Life is never quite the same after such a loss. One feels left, and pushed on into the front, out in the cold; but it is the divinely appointed way in which we are gradually to sever from this life, and prepare for the next, which is the real abiding life. You have your *own home* comforts, D.G. They will shine out all the brighter and more comforting now. God bless you all and comfort you.

CIX.

TO ONE OF HIS CLERGY—ON THE DEATH OF HIS WIFE.

LINCOLN, *December* 31, 1906.

Thank you so much for telling me yourself.

I always think of you as one of my first friends in the diocese, and I shall like to think now of the same little churchyard with still more precious memories. One by one they seem to be gathered in, generation after generation. It is hard sometimes to work with spirit, knowing how soon the work will pass to other hands, but really the work is not ours. We are only labourers in His vineyard, so we must try to do a good day's work each day, day by day.

And you, dear brother, will find it, I fear, far harder to have any heart for life; and yet *He* knows and feels for our sorrows, and can and will heal the broken-hearted, and give fresh gifts of faith and hope, so that you will have strength given you, I trust, and finish the work God prepared for you to do, and then will come re-union and rest.

That God may comfort and uphold you is the sincere prayer of yours very sincerely. . . .

CX.

TO A LADY—ON THE DEATH OF HER FATHER, AN OLD FRIEND OF THE BISHOP'S.

UPPER HOUSE OF CONVOCATION,
February 3, 1907.

Thank you very much for writing to tell me, though your letter has indeed been a great shock and grief to me. I did not know that my dear old friend was ill. We were so much together at first, and though we never met but seldom of late years, yet he was always the same and the bond of real affection was never broken. You will, I am sure, miss him very much. Indeed, it becomes very hard to keep a brave and cheerful interest in life when so many are leaving us. We must be thankful for the comfort of their love, and try and look forward and upward to the life above. This life seems to be the place for making friendships. The next, we hope, will be for enjoying them. I am writing this in the midst of the discussions of Convocation, as I did not like to let the day pass without writing. I shall be with you in spirit to-morrow.

May God guide, and support, and comfort you in your great loss.

CXI.

TO A LADY—ON THE DEATH OF HER MOTHER.

OLD PALACE, LINCOLN, *January* 11, 1909.

I must send you one word of sincere sympathy in the loss of your dear mother, for, though she had been spared to you for so many years, yet, when the time comes to leave, the loss is irreparable. It is a golden link broken with the past, and yet you have the best of comfort in this case when you look to the present and the future. Rest, and peace, and love, and light, all increasing to the perfect glory! We would not have it otherwise. R.I.P.

May God comfort you, and your good husband, and all around you.

CXII.

TO A LADY—ON THE DEATH OF HER FATHER.

LINCOLN, *June* 4, 1909.

I cannot tell you how much I feel for you all in the sudden reverse of your hopes.

I read your kind letter first (thank you very much for it), and among the other letters was one from Mr. ——, telling me all was over! Well, we know it is the Lord's doing, and your dear father would not wish us to wish it otherwise. I shall ever remember his beautiful, patient, trustful example all through your dear mother's illness, and his own long illness. It was wonderful how he continued his work. It always did me good to be with him, and I shall try and follow his example.

May God support, and comfort, and guide you. I am sure He will. Just rest quietly in His love, and in His own good time He will show you what you have to do, and then when your work is done you will look forward to joining again those who have gone before.

God bless you and keep you.

CXIII.

TO A FRIEND—ON THE DEATH OF HIS WIFE.

OLD PALACE, LINCOLN, *February* 9, 1910.

It is very kind of you to tell me yourself of your great sorrow and irreparable loss. May He, Who only can, support and comfort you. At first I can well believe the blow must be too crushing to allow us to do more than say "Thy Will be done." But in time, I hope, the brightness, and the wisdom, and love in which He ever acts, will appear through the darkness of the present cloud, and you will feel new strength to carry out the things that you have prayed over and planned together, so that your life will still have the consciousness of her presence helping you to persevere till you meet again.

That God may support and comfort you, and your family, is the sincere hope and prayer of yours sincerely.

CXIV.

TO ONE OF HIS CHAPLAINS—ON THE EXECUTION OF A CRIMINAL.

LINCOLN, *July* 17, 1891.

I want you, if you can, to pray for the poor thing, A—— S—— in the gaol here; he only has till Tuesday week. He is not at all hardened. He has been confirmed and a communicant often, and hopes to be on Sunday week. One cannot help feeling almost a desire to be hung or shot instead of being buried as if one was good.

I am sure the poor thing understands the Gospel and all that the Gospel was meant for. It is most helpful to see a man in the power of the faith facing death in good health and young. We don't do credit to the faith by living till the body falls to pieces through old age or disease.

Pardon all this, but *pray*. God bless you. . . .

CXV.

TO THE SAME.

LINCOLN, *July* 28, 1891.

Thank you indeed for thinking of *him* and me. It was most humbling. I had not the principal part to do this time; but we all hope the end was good. It is very terrible. I am very thankful that I was enabled to do the little that I did. Religion seemed to have plenty of strength, and to spare, in the midst of all those terrible surroundings.

But it is very awful, and one fears that one may be presumptuous. R.I.P.

CXVI.

TO THE SAME—ON THE EXECUTION OF ANOTHER CRIMINAL.

LINCOLN, *December* 4, 1893.

You have seen, I daresay, that we are in trouble here again. A poor dear Grimsby fisherman; it will all be over a fortnight to-morrow. Will you please remember him, H—— R——, and ask that he may be forgiven and accepted, and for me that my sins may not hinder my helping him. We have every hope for him, he is really most beautiful. I am just back from the gaol, so my hand shakes, but not for him; it is a great privilege if we are only equal to it. But you will remember poor Richard,[1] and understand that I cannot help asking God to hear his prayer for me now, if it be His Will. I think it is, it seems so easy.

With my love and blessing,

Always yours affectionately.

P.S.—Perhaps you could ask a few of the men to pray.[2]

1 The reference is to a criminal to whom he had ministered in a similar way seven years before.

2 His correspondent was at a Theological College.

LAST LETTERS.

CXVII.

TO AN OLD FRIEND WHO HAD HEARD THAT HE WAS NOT WELL.

LINCOLN, *October* 10, 1909.

Thanks for yours. Only old age! So, with rest, I may yet go on a bit. Give me your prayers, that I may be patient and thankful.

God bless you, dear child. Always your loving.

CXVIII.

IN REPLY TO ONE WHO HAD WRITTEN TO HIM ON HIS EIGHTIETH BIRTHDAY.

December 29, 1909.

It is wonderful indeed to have been preserved so long. My great fear is staying on to the injury of the Church. . . . Have you ever noticed the difference between the Prayer Book version and the Bible version of the 90th Psalm, verse 10. Instead of "We are gone" the Bible version is "We flee away." That is much brighter, and more suggestive of the truth of the continuous life.

The word for "Flee away" is the same as that used in Psalm 55, "Flee away and be at rest."

CXIX.

TO AN OLD FRIEND—IN REPLY TO A BIRTHDAY LETTER.

LINCOLN, *December* 31, 1909.

Thanks, dearest old child.
Don't forget me now to the end.

Always your loving.

Dear old Seymour! R.I.P.

CXX.

TO AN OLD FRIEND.

LINCOLN, *The Holy Innocents*, 1909.

It is very good of you to have remember me so long!

Thank you very much for your kind wishes. It is indeed wonderful how we have got on!

We must keep quietly to the old ways, and trust. The great comfort is knowing that the Church and the world are both under the eye and control of our Blessed Lord. He is Head over all and over the Church. One's only anxiety should be to know and do His Will, then calmly, thankfully, lovingly to trust.

With my love and blessing for the new year.

Believe me,
Always yours affectionately.

CXXI.

TO ONE OF HIS CLERGY.

LINCOLN, *February* 4, 1910.

I was very much disappointed in not being able to come to you for the Confirmation, but I have been unwell, and obliged to obey my doctor. I was glad to see what a nice number of candidates you had yourself, and very evenly balanced, boys and girls. I should have enjoyed being with you very much; but the great Gift is the same through whomsoever it is sent. The Bishop told me all went very well, but he was rather hurried at the end.

That God may continue to guide and bless your young people is the sincere prayer of yours. . . .

CXXII.

THE BISHOP'S LAST LETTER TO HIS DIOCESE; WRITTEN SIX DAYS BEFORE HE DIED.

OLD PALACE, LINCOLN, *March* 2, 1910.

I fear I am not able to write the letter I should wish to write. I have for some time been praying God to tell me when I should give up my work. Now He has sent me in His loving wisdom a clear answer. It is a very great comfort to me to be relieved from the responsibility of leaving you.

All I have to do is to ask you to forgive the many faults and innumerable shortcomings during the twenty-five years I have been with you, and ask you to pray God to perfect my repentance, and strengthen my faith to the end. All has been done in perfect love and wisdom.

My great wish has been to lead you to be Christlike Christians. In Christ is the only true hope of unity and peace. In Him we may be united to God and to one another.

May God guide and bless you all, and refresh you with the increasing consciousness of His Presence and His Love.

I am to the end,

Your friend and Bishop.

FRAGMENTS

I.

May, 1878.

The more I see of life the more wonderful it is, but it all points to this world being only the little short beginning. The real life we are all being prepared for is *above*. There we shall see the wisdom of our sorrows.

II.

July, 1877.

Thank you for your last kind letter. You must not over worry yourself about your advance in the Christian life. It is very simple, *the love of God* and *love of man*. That is perfection! Keep your *heart* with God, and then do the daily duties, and He will take care of you. He knows, and watches and leads us on. God bless you, dear —— and all yours, and fill you with His wisdom and holy love. . . .

III.

FLORENCE, *September*, 1888.

I think the two pictures that have helped me most are the round Botticelli and the Madonna del Cardellino in the Uffizi. The extreme purity of the beauty of the first is beyond any mere copy of the human, and the difference in the expression in the two Infants, the del Cardellino is still more suggestive of the Unseen.

The infant Baptist, you remember, is presenting the little bird, and evidently says: "Isn't it pretty." Like a simple child, the infant Saviour is pleased, but evidently says: "If you had seen what I have, and if you knew what I have to go through." It is a most helpful and *yon*-side picture.

IV.

AFTER DR. LIDDON'S FUNERAL.

September, 1890.

It was a great comfort having you with me, and I trust will prove an historic link for you with Mr. Keble, and Dr. Pusey, and the Tractarian standpoint.

We shall need to stand firm, but God can save by many or by few.

It was most wonderful! I hope I shall never forget the welcome of those faces as the coffin floated on towards them.

V.

February, 1892.

If Bishops could only be in Retreat for nine months (with the Book of Leviticus[1]), and were confirming for the other three, the candidates would go straight to Paradise. They are most lovely. I do wish you had been with me. I never can be thankful enough for such a refreshing day. If we could only do it decently!

VI.

August, 1893.

The purely evidential man seems to me like men who are for ever studying Bradshaw, but never making a start. What I hope rather to do now is (D.V.) to spend what remains in trying to understand what it is to be a Christian. I think it ought to be the remedy for a great many of our bothers, and make us restful, and hopefully happy, with a simple sense of freedom, and with a royal beauty and courage.

VII.

April, 1894.

I love sitting in my chair by the window. It is *too delicious!* I must really try to be more restful, and spend all my time in giving thanks for all the great goodness which God has given me. I do hope

1 The book he happened to be reading devotionally at the time.

there is some real Evolena-like progress in the Church of England—that spirit of restful dignified contentment which ought to mark all true Churchpeople. I am sure you must be seeing something of it in your own little village.

VIII.

September, 1894.

. . . . I feel decidedly better—refreshed and stronger—and that desire to do things much better, which is such a refreshing and sustaining gift, and as long as one can hope to improve one can work.

IX.

January, 1896.

When I think of all God's mercies to me I am ashamed of my want of trustfulness and cheerfulness. Old age is beginning to be a reality, and it seems to require special help. I sometimes fear whether one ought not to give up work and attend to oneself more. Perhaps that will be settled for me.

X.

February, 1897.

I wonder how our good friends at Evolena are? I constantly think of their simple out-of-the-world life, and it seems to me the highest. I suppose we ought not to run away from where we are placed; but I am sure we lose a great deal in losing simplicity. We had a magnificent exhibition of simplicity and resting in the Archbishop's[1] speech at Canterbury at the luncheon after the Enthronement. Did you read it? He is magnificently simple.

XI.

October, 1897.

Sometimes I long for rest, but I believe if one had more faith, and trusted to one's daily bread to give strength for the daily duties, one would have power enough. To be thankful in looking back over the past, and content and cheerful in the present, and trustful and hopeful in looking to the future, is what I am trying to aim at.

XII.

S. John the Baptist, 1901.

Ah! how many precious memories your kind visit awoke. How can I ever be thankful enough for the blessings I received through you all at Cuddesdon! Do not forget me in your prayers, that I may be faithful to the end.

1 Temple.

XIII.

November, 1901.

How wonderful the goodness and loving-kindness of God is! "Like as a father pitieth his own children." I suppose you can understand that better than I can, but it does seem wonderful the certainty of the love to go back to, again and again. Good-bye, dear friend; don't forget me. I shall need your prayers more and more now to the end, and don't forget to pray for me after that, that God may continue to do for me what He will know I shall need.

XIV.

TO DEAN LUCKOCK—AFTER A VISIT TO LICHFIELD.

August, 1902.

I must send you one word of thanks for my very pleasant and helpful visit, and all your great kindness. It was very wonderful to *see* a cathedral coming out into the full expansion of its many-sided power in the services, and the building, and the college, and the life in it, and through it, making its impression on the city and neighbourhood.

XV.

November, 1902.

I still go on in my simple superficial way, loving flowers, and birds, and the sunlight on the apples, and the sunset, and like to think more and more of the verse "With Thee is the well of life, and in Thy light shall we see light." And so again: "Thou openest Thine hand and fillest all things living with plenteousness." The flowers and the birds, and angels and men, all things that are!!

I feel more and more how utterly superficial one's knowledge is, but it seems, D.G., to be in the right direction, and to be more and more attractive, and I hope, please God, is leading one nearer to the One Beginning and End of all.

XVI.

April, 1906.

It is so good of you to be so true and such a delight! The longer one lives the more one values true friends! I like to think of this world as the place for making friends, and the next for enjoying them! I sometimes am troubled when I think how little I have seen of old Cuddesdon men, but, please God, when we meet in Paradise, it will all come back again, and then go on and on, as Dr. Pusey used to like to translate the Hebrew word for eternity, "For *ever*, AND YET!"

XVII.

October, 1906.

It is hard sometimes to keep brightly on with so many of the old supports and comforts removed, but we know "Power belongeth unto God," and He can put it forth in the way that is best. We want more faith, and hope, and love, and to turn more to His mercy and loving-kindness, which every year seems more wonderful.

XVIII.

AFTER THE ANNUAL VISIT TO THE BISHOP AT THE OLD PALACE, LINCOLN, OF THE MEMBERS OF ELY THEOLOGICAL COLLEGE,

Ascension Day, 1907.

Many, many thanks, dearest child. I am glad you got safe back. It was very refreshing having you all. As Milman said of a visit to Cuddesdon: "It was like a breath from the Garden of Eden before the door was shut." My love and blessing to all.

XIX.

Undated.

I am so sorry you are not well, especially your throat, for just now it is most important to *read* LOUD and make as much *noise* as we can in the *service*, and not be creeping about in a mousey saintly way.

XX.

January, 1908.

Thank you so much for your loving words:
"He loved them *to the end!*"
This is our standard!
I was seventy-eight two Sundays ago! So you must keep up your love a little longer, and then in Paradise it will (D.V.) be like Cuddesdon again.

XXI.

August, 1908.

I have always had a real sympathy for the Wesleyans and Primitives as people who wish to be good, but I do not believe we shall win them by giving away our Apostolical and Catholic position.